God Knows
We Get
Angry

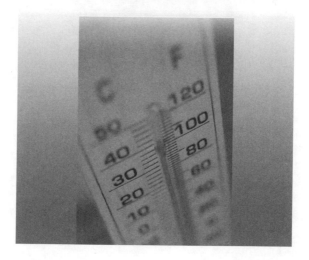

God Knows You're Stressed:
Simple Ways to Restore Your Balance

God Knows You'd Like a New Body:
12 Ways to Befriend the One You've Got

God Knows You're Grieving:
Things to Do to Help You Through

God Knows Marriage Isn't Always Easy:
Twelve Ways to Add Zest

God Knows We Get Angry

Healthy ways to deal with it

Priscilla J. Herbison

SORIN BOOKS   Notre Dame, Indiana

As Publisher of the GOD KNOWS series, SORIN BOOKS is dedicated to providing resources to assist readers to enhance their quality of life. We welcome your comments and suggestions, which may be conveyed to:

SORIN BOOKS
P.O. Box 1006
Notre Dame, IN 46556-1006
Fax: 1-800-282-5681

© 2002 by Priscilla Herbison

www.sorinbooks.com

International Standard Book Number: 1-893732-33-9

Cover photograph © 2001 Stanley Brown/Tony Stone

Cover design by Katherine Robinson Coleman

Text design by Brian C. Conley

Printed and bound in the United States of America.

Library of Congress Cataloging-in-Publication Data
Herbison, Priscilla.
    God knows we get angry : healthy ways to deal with it / Priscilla Herbison.
        p. cm.
    ISBN 1-893732-33-9 (pbk.)
    1. Anger--Religious aspects--Christianity.   I. Title.
    BV4627.A5 H47 2002
    248.8'6--dc21
                                                2001005306
                                                CIP

BV
4627
.A5
H47
2002

CONTENTS

Introduction

One of the joys of writing a book, the saying goes, is that you get to write yourself into knowledge. Forgiveness is a topic that I thought was as familiar to me as the burl on the handle of a well-worn jackknife.

Anger, on the other hand, was something I had to become reacquainted with. Or, so I thought. I was wrong. Throughout the writing of this book, I found myself on a voyage of discovery.

Once I worked through the many levels of anger, I soon discovered that forgiveness may be more nuanced and multi-layered than is anger.

Moreover, as a writer and as a teacher, I have always loved paradox and metaphor. The discovery of layers of paradox in both anger and forgiveness comes out in nature as well as our behavior: body, mind, and soul. For instance, I discovered, to my delight, the original meaning of my grandfather's American Indian name, "Ah-ne-way-we-dung." It means "the sound of thunder going away." Like the sound of anger rolled away by forgiveness or kindness! His name could be a metaphor for this book, just as his stories show the way to release anger and discover the transforming power of forgiveness.

In addition to the discovery of stories, I reveled in finding apt quotes for you, the reader, and me as a writer to enjoy. One is a French-Arab proverb: "Write injuries in the sand, kindness in marble." This quote guided me as I found a working definition of anger as well as one of forgiveness to serve as a backdrop for this book.

7

Anger, I discovered, is a natural emotion designed to protect us from imminent danger or harm. We need it when we are infants or else we wouldn't survive. We need it as we grow older to protect ourselves from assaults on our integrity and dignity as human beings. It is the repression of anger that eats away at the marble. Repressed anger shoots out as hostility, rage, and destruction, and turns relationships into dust. Repressed anger has the effect of defending us so completely that it obscures our true selves, repels intimacy, and locks us in.

The way to break free from this vise of anger is learned through honest, direct expression of anger. It's this honesty that invites intimacy. It honors ourselves. It respects the other as an equal partner.

I've learned how hard it is to befriend anger. It is especially hard for some women in our culture to learn. Men seem to have an easier time with anger, though maybe not forgiveness. In any case, we have something to teach each other, and we can learn to release anger in a potent way.

I've also discovered that, at the right time and in a way that honors our integrity, forgiveness is as liberating as it is transforming. The Dalai Lama gave the most simple, radiant definition of forgiveness when he said in an ecumenical dialogue, "Forgiveness is simply suspending ill-will toward another who has caused you pain." The same could be said of a situation that hurt you.

Forgiveness is luminous. It is like iridescent sand that softens the contours and makes our passageway more gentle as we walk toward the dawn of a new day.

Forgiveness is powerful. Only the strong can summon it. In time, like the undulating sands of the desert or waves on a glacial cliff, it will wear away the hardest, sharpest surface.

Finally, I discovered a series of exercises and meditations that I've included to help you and I process the levels of anger and forgiveness. You may want to select some just for yourself as they move you. You may want to invite a partner or friend to engage in the exercises together to discover new ways that honestly and directly affirm your true self.

Special Thanks

I now understand how any writing cannot come into being without the support and encouragement of others. To the reader, my prayer for you is that you have such friends on your life's journey. Thanks to Carl Koch, without whose strong editing, guidance, and affirmation this book would not exist. To Janet Marinelli, Sharon Votel, Carole Gesme, and Nan Stevenson for their suggestions and critical reading, thanks, too.

The stories in this work are true. With three exceptions, I have changed the identities of the characters, so any resemblance to anyone living or deceased is coincidental. The three exceptions are my father, Charles Wesley Herbison, whose character is so deeply etched in my memory, it would be impossible to invent a fictional likeness; my lovely sister Judith, who has given her permission for my short sketch of her during our childhood; and me.

Working with anger and the desire to forgive is transforming work. Forgiveness is the catalyst to transform our world. But we won't be able to arrive at true forgiveness until we acknowledge and embrace our anger. It is hard work, but worthy of our time, patience, reflection, and heart.

The hard work of moving from anger to forgiveness, but also the wonderful rewards, came home to me when my friend, Ed Colon, shared this story with me:

"I'm sick of him. He's a good-for-nothing, a total screw up, and that's all he'll ever be."

My father's words, coming from a face twisted and ugly in anger, cut right through me. It was only one of many judgments meted out by him during my adolescence. What little self-esteem I had shattered into jagged pieces that wounded me in every corner of my being. Later on, I cried without restraint as I sat in the company of my best friend. I was in college at the time and on my way in the world. Yet, my father still hurt me, as he had done many times throughout my childhood. I had yet to please him or earn his respect, regardless of how much I tried. My hurt turned to anger that affected my health and boiled over into other relationships.

As I grew older, my father and I settled into a relationship of tolerance and conditional acceptance. It was conditional in that I remained vigilant for any slight or hurt which would again fan the flames of my deep-seated anger.

With age, I gradually came to understand my father's own troubled beginnings and lack of parental love. Underneath all of the bravado and anger was a scared and insecure man. Now in the sunset of his life, he began to reflect on his life and mistakes in rearing me. Writing to me, he explained:

Certain events in the last couple of years have caused me to come to the conclusion that life is short and there are many things that we should do while we have the opportunity. I know I made serious errors. I was so determined to make sure that you learned everything my way that I almost ruined you. I'm asking you to forgive the many errors I made. Forgive me for the warm embraces that I never gave to you and therefore never got in return. You are my only son and everything I could have hoped for. I love you because you are what you are and because of what you have given to me.

My father and I finally began to enjoy each other as confidants and friends. Our reconciliation was cemented when my father made a rare trip from his home in Los Angeles to visit my family in Minnesota. I watched with great joy as he bounced his grandchildren on his knee, laughing and smiling as I had never seen before. We talked, reminisced, and tried to make up some of the time we lost. Having forgiven one another, we both recognized with sadness and regret the years of antipathy that separated us.

Within weeks of saying goodbye, my father died of congestive heart failure. He was a good man, who strove to love and be loved. However, like many of us, he was wounded. The tragedy of his life was that he lived most of it often defeating his own efforts at happiness, a fate that I was determined to not repeat.

My father's harsh words to me as an adolescent were forgiven, and I thought, a thing of the past. However, they had burned themselves on my psyche and became a part of who

I was. Now, the voice of diminishment wasn't my father's, but my own. As a child, I had internalized those hurtful words all too well. His judgments were now mine, only they were well hidden behind the adult defenses of denial, projection, and justification. Taking those defenses into my work and family life, I knew that I had inherited the legacy of my father's wounds.

Once, when I was yelling at my nine-year-old son, I could see the hurt and dismay in his eyes. In a moment of painful remembrance, I felt like I was yelling at myself as a little boy. I had become like my father, and knew it was time to seek help.

I've been in therapy for several years now fighting the depression I have felt since my father died. It has been a long hard road of self-forgiveness, acceptance, and healing. I am less driven by anxiety, fears, and expectations now, and am happier and more relaxed. Like a precious vase that has been broken and bears the scar of a repair along its face, I will always be the bearer of my wounds and history. However, I am learning to love those wounds, as well as other people I encounter on my journey who also seek to be more human in their brokenness.

The grace of the difficult years of my adulthood was to be able to see myself and others more clearly. In so doing, I feel God in acceptance and love of all that I am, enabling me to share that acceptance and love with a growing circle of people in my life.

It is good to be where I stand today, but the journey continues and there are more challenges ahead.

Forgiveness is only one step on the path to healing and wholeness—stay on the journey.

Yes, let's stay on the journey.

W A Y   1 :

Be Angry!

LET US SPEAK THE TRUTH TO OUR
NEIGHBORS, FOR WE ARE MEMBERS
OF ONE ANOTHER.

BE ANGRY BUT DO NOT SIN; DO
NOT LET THE SUN GO DOWN ON
YOUR ANGER.

Paul of Tarsus

In order to make our way toward forgiveness, we almost always have to start by being angry. As paradoxical as it sounds, being with our anger actually makes forgiveness possible. Anger is energy. Suppressed or denied, the energy can destroy other people and us. When faced and accepted, the energy can move us toward forgiveness and life. Examining anger should help explain its energy and its relationship to forgiveness.

If the opening passage from the Bible surprises you as it did me, it may mean that—like me—you have been taught and shaped by your family or your faith community or your teachers that anger is one of the seven deadly sins. And as a sin, anger was to be avoided at all

15

costs. You were also to avoid persons and situations that would trigger it. So, you reigned anger in and learned to suppress anger. Or you may have learned other words and phrases for the feelings that surged when you experienced some unpleasant or painful event, like "disappointment" or "hurt" or "surprised about inappropriate behavior."

But as I read Paul's advice, it's clear that he was bold about proclaiming his emotions. He didn't repress or deny his anger. He named it for what it is. Anger is a God-given, strong, energizing emotion that reacts to an unpleasant, painful, or threatening external event. Paul, Jesus, Gandhi, Martin Luther King, Jr., and other great spiritual leaders were able to harness the energy of anger to change the world around them—to make it a better place, to let others know they were hurt, to improve relationships, and to prevent behavior that could destroy others.

This kind of anger is positive, life-giving, pulsating, exciting, healthy, even holy. To paraphrase writer Mary Gordon, when you're angry you know you're truly alive. This is natural anger. It's distinguishable from hostility or indirect anger that tears apart relationships and wreaks our health—our very lives. Hostility is sneaky. Unlike anger, which is an emotion, hostility is a persistent negative attitude toward others or situations that can attach to the emotion of anger and escalate into hatred, aggression, and even violence.

Repressed, indirect anger is also subtle. Because it's so buried or denied, it surfaces at the most inopportune moments and is often directed at the wrong person or target.

Take our self-sacrificing moments when we feel ignored by family or colleagues and say something like, "Oh, I'm really nobody special. I don't deserve a parking space." Or consider the single relative who tells her family when they go out of town to celebrate a holiday, "Don't worry about me. I'll just microwave a frozen dinner and watch TV. I'll think of something." These are examples of passive anger, usually manifested in sarcasm, the cold shoulder, low-blow remarks, or blame.

Anger need not be explosive, but can find nasty expression in remarks like: "Mary's always getting it wrong, but she isn't the sharpest knife in the drawer." This non-integrated anger combines passivity and aggression, causing embarrassment or humiliation in others and us.

Anger's manifestations can be subtle. A person who resents always hosting family dinners almost unconsciously burns the meal. A disaffected relative comes chronically late for family get-togethers. Actions like chronic overspending can also be expressions of deeply hidden anger.

Hidden or indirect anger doesn't look like anger. It can start with a question, "Can we do a reality check here?" and end up with grousing about a third person. Murray Bowen, the pioneer theorist in family systems, called this *triangulation*. Triangulation happens when instead of going directly to the person we're angry with and leveling with them, we complain about that person to someone we think will sympathize with us or even side with us. Such triangulation can polarize families and organizations. It's just the opposite of Paul's direct approach from the scriptures.

So where do we learn these negative messages about anger? As children, we're sent messages about expressing our anger through the gestures, voice, and the example of significant adults. As we grow older, our school, neighborhood, gender identity, and faith community may reinforce these messages.

The truth is that anger as an emotion is neutral. Indeed, we need anger for survival. When an infant is hungry or in pain, they will scream angrily for care and attention. If they don't get it, they will die. This fatal condition has a name: failure to thrive. Anger is also an appropriate response to being ignored, ridiculed, or rejected. If there's no response, the spirit will be crushed. If we hold anger in, we run the risk of physical and emotional illness.

Anger sends us messages that we need to hear. We may need to act ON anger, but we don't need to act it OUT. So, the road to forgiveness begins by being angry—angry without shame, guilt, or fear.

IT'S MY RULE TO NEVER LOSE ME TEMPER 'TIL IT WOULD BE DETRIMENTAL TO KEEP IT.

Sean O'Casey

Be Angry!

- Recall early messages that you received about anger and dealing with anger. Did these help you appropriately deal with your anger?
- Try these exercises to see if you can identify and acknowledge anger:
  - Describe what anger looks like to you. Maybe draw a picture of it or write a story describing it.

- What three things are most likely to trigger your anger?

- Imagine one of the three things that trigger your anger happening to you. How do you feel?

- Pretend you look at a videotape or a photo of an event during which you became exceedingly angry. Express your reaction. This lets you be prepared instead of surprised by it. Stop action: reverse. Try out different ways of responding. Draw three long breaths and carry on!

- Recall a time when you had every right to be angry, but you hid it even from yourself. You suppressed it. Did you make sneak attacks, snide remarks, and bitter asides? Did denying your anger lead to inappropriate actions on your part that ended up being humiliating or even destructive for you?

- Write out your anger. Studies have shown that just writing down our feelings and descriptions of events can relieve considerable stress and lower blood pressure besides. Put pen to paper and write. Begin an entry with something like:

  When she did . . . I really got angry, and. . . .

  Then just keep writing.

- Paul says not to let the sun go down on our anger; sound advice. If you are angry about something right now, sit with it awhile, write it out, or offer it up to the universe or to God. Take some deep breaths and, as you breathe out slowly and fully, let the anger out too.

- If something is making you angry, how can you use that energy for the good? Is your anger calling you to make some situation better? If there is no clear way to make that situation better, use your anger-energy to do some random act of kindness for someone who needs your assistance.

WHEN WE BRING ANGER INTO THE
AREA WHERE WE CAN RESPOND TO
IT . . . IT EMERGES INTO THE LIGHT
OF OUR WHOLENESS. THEN EVEN
ANGER DOES NOT CLOSE OUR
HEART. THEN ANGER IS NO LONGER
A HINDRANCE BUT A PROFOUND
TEACHER.

Stephen Levine

Confession

I was wreathed in shame and anger. That alone was enough to goad me to the confessional on my short Easter break visit back to Minnesota that sunny Saturday afternoon. I was convinced that anger of the depth I felt was enough to put me in hell; except I already felt like I was in hell.

Just three weeks before, I'd become engaged to a man I'd known for over a year. I had been deeply in love and overjoyed about the prospect of marriage and a family. It seemed like a heaven-sent match. We were both committed to civil rights and social justice during those halcyon days of the late 60s. The best part, from my point of view, was that Sam and I were members of the same faith community.

Best of all, Sam was funny, artistic, and animated when we were together. Communication is essential in any relationship. For me it takes on greater weight because of my hearing impairment. A birth trauma left me with some residual hearing ability. Early medical and speech therapy interventions give me an ability to read speech at about a forty-two percent accuracy rate. Any interference makes it hard for me to connect to a conversation. To my joy and relief, Sam seemed to care that I was always included.

As the months went on in our courtship, there were some fitful moments. Despite these, I was sure everything would turn out well in the end. It was not to be.

After our engagement was announced, our relationship started to run aground. Once, at a late night party, I made a teasing remark to Sam. His reaction was rage, and he punched me in my shoulder to emphasize it. His best friend, Dave, was standing nearby and came running over to my side. I was in shock.

Sam started apologizing, saying he didn't mean it, he just got out of hand, didn't know his own strength and it wouldn't happen again.

Later the next day, Dave called and asked if I could meet him for coffee. I did. Any thought I'd had that we were going to talk about the wedding plans evaporated as soon as I saw Dave's somber face.

"Trudy [Dave's wife] and I were talking about you and Sam last night," he started slowly. "We both think so much of you and we think you need to know about Sam. But we think you should have a frank talk with him, not us."

Dave rushed on, "You see, he's changed a lot since we were all kids growing up. We thought he'd matured a lot. But, we really think you need to ask why he left college."

I felt like molten lead had just been poured into my stomach. I tried to get some sense of what it was from Dave, but that was all he'd share. I really wanted to just ignore Dave and Trudy's worries. But their sincerity and urgency matched my growing unease.

I met Sam after work and got straight to the question. He gave two different versions, one more standard than the other. These versions didn't square with previous stories he'd told me about those days. What made it worse was his rapid-fire delivery and falling into an accent made his words hard for me to follow. I tried to clarify what he was saying and, as I did, one of the links that had drawn us together snapped apart.

Sam began to mock me. He started repeating one of my stock ways of asking someone to repeat something I can't hear, let alone understand. His mouth turned downward into a sneer. "Thory," he lisped, "tho' thorry. . . . What? What? Do you know how it drives everyone crazy to have to repeat things to you all the time? I'm sick of it! Can you hear that?"

By now he was shouting so loud that my neighbor called through the wall, "What in hell's going on?"

Sam punched the wall with his fist twice and cussed me out.

I didn't know if Sam meant this for the neighbor or for me, but it didn't matter. I swept past him, opened the door to the common hall, and commanded, "It's over. You can leave."

Sam grabbed his coat. "Don't worry, I'm leaving, and you, don't think you'll ever marry. You're cursed. No one would ever put up with you!"

At that moment, my only feeling was relief. I stayed with friends, changed the locks on my doors, and made arrangements to go home for the upcoming holiday weekend. The shame crept in when I thought about all the unraveling of wedding plans that had to be done.

When I called my parents to tell them to stop the wedding plans, I was surprised when my dad blurted out, "I'm glad you're coming home, kid, just what did you ever see in that. . . ." He didn't get a chance to pour it on because my mother pulled the phone away. For her part, she was remarkably kind and insightful. We made plans for the weekend visit.

I remained furious about Sam's betrayal and dishonesty. I felt taken advantage of. And I was angry about the mockery. My openness and vulnerability, the sharing of my innermost feelings and thoughts, my attempts to understand him were flung in my face. Even more, I began to worry about whether my attempts to get clarity were really as irritating to others as Sam had said. I began to loathe myself. My anger and self-loathing oscillated with my pity for him.

I kept remembering what Dave had said once, "No matter what happens, just know that Sam is so attracted to your goodness, he really needs that." I felt like I was trying to stabilize a glider in a gale. The glider was in a descent to hell. This was the state I was in when I arrived at my parents' home—guilt at my anger, shame at the betrayal, self-loathing, and fury at Sam.

I decided to meet with one of the ministers at my church. It turned out that I was given an appointment with Joe, the son of an old family friend. My first impulse was to bolt. Despite the guarantee of anonymity, the prospect of revealing this shameful sin to a family friend gave me pause. But there was this. Joe's whole posture was one of respect and absolute attention. I knew that I could hear him, and he me. So I plunged ahead.

When I finished, Joe startled me by his response. He said, "There's no sin here. You were in an abusive relationship. You have every right to be angry!"

He must have seen the amazement on my face because he continued, "Jesus was angry, and for good reason. He was angry when he told Peter to stop dancing in attendance around him, wanting to make a monument to him, or when he drove moneychangers out of the temple. You're given that gift of anger too. It's for your own self-protection, for survival, and dignity. Admit that you're angry. The sin comes in denying it and not being the person you really are, a daughter of God."

DON'T START WITH AN APOLOGY. WHEN YOU PREFACE EVERYTHING WITH, "I'M SORRY". . . . IT PUTS YOU IN A DIMINISHED POSITION! TELL THE TRUTH, HOW YOU FEEL . . . . IF THEY CAN'T DEAL WITH HONESTY, LEAVE 'M TO HEAVEN!

Fernando Colon

The Law of Kindness

I was admitted to the second year of law school on probation. My grades were marginal in large part because, due to my hearing impairment, it was impossible for me to follow the classroom give-and-take in what was then considered the Socratic method of teaching the law.

I was allowed to tape lectures and have an interpreter present in the classroom. Another accommodation was that I was assigned an acoustically sound, enclosed carrel in the library where I could transcribe lectures. One day in early September as I sat transcribing an evidence lecture, my door vibrated from hard, incessant knocks. The hard rap on my door was the librarian's signal for a fire alert. I opened the door, ready to evacuate, but was blocked by two women classmates, Sue and Mary, standing shoulder to shoulder. "We're here to tell you to turn off that tape recorder," one of them said.

My embarrassment and apology turned to ice when the other woman added, "Anyway, how did you get this carrel? Only law review and moot court students get these, and we both know you don't deserve it!"

I started explaining that I needed it for sound acoustics, but was cut off by her raised palm. Mary continued, "We've submitted an appeal to the library staff. You have no right to be here. You're taking the space of someone who deserves it." They turned on their heels and left as quickly as they'd come.

I stood rooted to the floor, fighting conflicting thoughts. One of self-doubt: "They're right, I don't have their ability to get on law review." The other with angry retaliation: "I wish just for one day they were hearing impaired." I kept vacillating between hurt and anger until I finally realized that I wasn't getting anywhere. I did have a right to be there. I decided that if I was going to make it through the second year and the third, I had to have a level playing field. I needed the accommodations. Energy I didn't know I had surged through me. I was without a doubt, angry!

With that I flew down the stairs. Carrie, the head librarian, was standing in her office, legs planted like posts, and arms folded across her chest, gazing directly at me. I drew three long breaths and tried to keep my voice level to not betray my anger.

"We seem to have a problem with the carrel assignment." She waited, saying nothing. "According to Mary and Sue, my transcribing tapes in the carrel is causing a disturbance for them. I regret that." Still she said nothing.

"There are two other parts to this problem," I continued. "In their opinion, this is designated for law review or moot court students only. I am neither. The other part of the problem is that I continue to need a soundproof acoustical space for transcription of lecture tapes."

Carrie continued to look impassive as she began to speak. "They came by with their complaint. They're wrong about the carrel assignments. The library staff makes that designation with everyone's, and I mean everyone's, needs in mind. Still, they could be right about the acoustics."

She promised to talk to the new library director, Dr. Theil, and get back to me. "Can you come back in two hours? We'll have an answer by then." I could, and I did.

When I saw her, it was clear that she was trying not to smile. "Dr. Theil is giving you her office. It's absolutely soundproof, and it's in the faculty section away from the student area. Here's an elevator key so you can get clear access."

I was as grateful as I was astounded. "But," I stammered, "where will Dr. Theil go?"

"Oh, not to worry," Carrie replied. "She's taking your old carrel and the one next to it for research. She wants to keep an eye on the students."

"One more thing," Carrie said—and now I did see a glint in her eye. "She says you can keep the office until you finish your Ph.D., for all she cares!"

My anger had been swept away by this kindness. And any shame or doubt or guilt at being angry had gone too. Now I could put my energy back where it belonged, studying law.

Happily, only a wry feeling of irony instead of resentment crossed my mind some years later when our alumni magazine featured Sue and Mary as partners in a large corporate firm. They had just co-authored an article advising employers about insulating themselves from employment discrimination litigation.

I HAVE A RIGHT TO MY ANGER,

AND I DON'T WANT ANYBODY

TELLING ME I SHOULDN'T BE,

THAT IT'S NOT NICE TO BE,

AND THAT SOMETHING'S WRONG

WITH ME BECAUSE I GET ANGRY.

Audre Lourde

Claim Your Anger and Your Power

IT WAS YOU WHO FORMED MY
INWARD PARTS; YOU KNIT ME
TOGETHER IN MY MOTHER'S WOMB.
I PRAISE YOU, [GOD], FOR I AM
FEARFULLY AND WONDERFULLY
MADE.

The Psalms

One of the most moving scenes in John Steinbeck's *The Grapes of Wrath* is built around the birth of a child. When the father holds his baby for the first time, he gazes upon its downy head and says, what I think most parents at some time or another have said about their child, "For you, it will be different." Different usually means a better world for the child to grow up in.

For a moment, imagine what it would be like if, on a perfect July morning, the sky was azure blue, the air was warm, and a gentle northwest breeze brushed your cheek. The delicate perfume of daisy and buttercups drifted in the breeze beside a limestone brick walkway as your mother and dad brought you home from the hospital for the first time.

As you are carried in the front door of your home, you are greeted by adoring brothers and sisters who are so proud of you and whose only wish is to support and cherish you all your days as they are already doing for each other. After you've grown older, you are welcomed into a community of faith where you will continue to learn lessons your family is already teaching you, that you are a child of the Creator in whose image you are fearfully and wonderfully made. In a few more years, you enter a school where your teacher's primary goal is to draw forth the talents you were given to make the world an even better place. Your community government and organizations exist for freedom, tranquility, and the pursuit of happiness. Your lifelong friends are known for their kindness and laughter. You take delight in each other's accomplishments and give freely so no one is wanting. Your workplace is filled with positive energy, compassion, and building of the community. And, when it is all done, your friends and your family meet at your bedside as you make your final journey home to where you first began, into the arms of your Creator.

If you read this far, how do you react to this imaginative tale? Does some of it at least intrigue you, make you wistful? Or does it turn you off and make you feel like gagging? If so, you may agree with the slogan I once saw on a T-shirt on campus that proclaimed, "Life is hard, mean, and rude . . . then you die." Your reaction is likely one of incredulity.

Then again, most of us want to experience or have experienced a taste of love and happiness. Yet, even in the most loving of homes, we experience hurt. We carry the scars of rejection, betrayal, disappointments, and abandonment.

Where do the anger and its concomitant suffering come from? And where do they go? Trappist monk Thomas Keating suggests that the happiness we seek, the happiness described in fable is the happiness of our true self, the self that is in complete intimacy with the Creator who made us. Our uniqueness is an expression of the divine life within us.

If this is so, why have we experienced suffering, and particularly, the suffering caused by anger? If we look to the Bible, it teaches that any substitute for God—demons or false gods—that would lure us away from journeying with the Holy One are sure to bring great suffering.

The early Christian writer Augustine of Hippo concluded that one of the sources of suffering and anger is ignorance. Ignorance means that we are looking for happiness and peace, but we're clueless as to how to find it. Another source is concupiscence. In the words of a popular country song, concupiscence is, "Looking for love [or happiness] in all the wrong places." Buddhism—indeed most of the great religious traditions—has similar teachings about suffering and anger.

Psychology supports what the religious traditions have known too. We are not born with self-consciousness, and we are not conscious of the total experience of God. Therefore, we rely on certain biological needs: survival and security needs, then power and control needs, and finally, affection or esteem needs. Without these instinctual needs, we probably wouldn't survive infancy. As a result, by nature we judge everything that enters into our universe on whether it can meet these needs.

As with the rat in E. B. White's story *Charlotte's Web*, we ask, "What's in it for me?" When we're little, if any of our biological needs aren't met, if our drives for security, control, or affection aren't fulfilled, the unbearable pain can drive the suffering into our unconscious. We shove our pain deep into our unconscious to be rid of it. But there is a problem here.

Our body holds these memories and they manifest themselves as ulcers, headaches, hypertension, or rashes. They strike out as overt anger, or passive aggression, or emerge in indirect expressions such as sarcasm, sharp teasing, chronic lateness, burning the family meals, or depression. Repressed anger can have addictive expressions in such things as food, computer games, sex, and drugs, including alcohol.

In post-toddler years, we start to drink in the values and norms, biases, and prejudices of our family, religion, school, nationality, gender, race, and sexual orientation. "The combination of these forces, the drive for happiness in the form of security and survival, affection and esteem, and power and control, and over identification with a particular group to which we belong greatly complicates our emotional program for happiness," says Keating. The drive to meet our unconscious needs and over-identification with a group fuel our delusions of what brings happiness and creates monsters we must fight to achieve them.

The single most effective way of dealing with these fearful and wonderful instinctual drives is self-knowledge. Our automatic impulses and knee-jerk reactions to threats to our security, self-esteem, and power need not push us along. The more we understand and accept our basic needs, the less likely we are to hurl ourselves angrily at the monsters that we perceive threatening us. We can stop blaming others for our suffering and banish from our vocabulary phrases like, "They made me do it! It's all their fault."

When we claim our anger and the sources of this anger, we gradually live within our true self, the fearful and wonderful self that the Creator made. If we don't claim the sources of our anger, suffering and bitterness will hold us hostage. Until we discover and accept our true self—with its desires for security, power, and self-esteem—the one that is made for happiness and love will need to wait in the wings for the false self to get off center stage.

FREEDOM IS . . . OUR CAPACITY TO MOLD OURSELVES. FREEDOM IS THE OTHER SIDE OF CONSCIOUSNESS OF SELF: IF WE WERE NOT ABLE TO BE AWARE OF OURSELVES, WE WOULD BE PUSHED ALONG BY INSTINCT OR THE AUTOMATIC MARCH OF HISTORY, LIKE BEES OR MASTODONS.

Rollo May

Claim Your Anger and Your Power

- In order to identify the source of our anger, it's useful to figure out whether our desire to control a situation, our need for security, or our desire for affection or esteem is being threatened. Identify a situation in the past week in which anger welled up in you. Bring the situation clearly to mind. Then ponder these questions and, perhaps, write your responses:

- What was the initial internal cause?

- What did you perceive was threatened: your need for security or survival; control or power; or desire for affection or esteem?

- The following exercise is suggested by William A. Menninger, a monk, writer, and teacher:

  - Looking at the same situation of anger asked for above, does this incident remind you of a time in your youth or childhood when you were wounded?

  - Can you make a statement about this? For example, "I am angry about my son taking the car while I was gone on the weekend. Why does this make me angry? Does it threaten my security? (Probably not.) Does it threaten my sense of esteem? (Maybe he doesn't think much of me if he runs off with my car.) Does it threaten my control? (Absolutely!)"

  - Then consider: Is this worth giving up my need or desire for control or power; esteem or affection; security or survival?

  - If you can do this, you are, as Menninger suggests, not giving power over to your son or giving up correcting him. What you're doing is letting go of the anger that has ahold of you as you go about teaching him to "do the right thing."

- Sit in a comfortable chair. Gently breathe in and breathe out three times. Hold your right hand with your left hand (opposite if your dominant hand is your left hand) and bring your right hand to the place in your body where you either feel blockage or hurt. As you cup your hand gently over the place where you find hurt, hold it as you would a bird or little baby and say, "I will not abandon you, I am here to help and to listen."

  If there was trauma, be sure to do this exercise with a professional counselor. If you find the hurt is too intense, tell your body, "I am not abandoning you, I am going to get help (a counselor) and I am coming back to be with you."

- Find a quiet place. Relax by breathing slowly and deeply, stretching any stiff muscles from head to toe. Then, in harmony with your breathing, repeat this simple affirmation: "I am fearfully, wonderfully made. I claim my anger and my power."

THE ORIGINAL SIN THAT AFFECTS VIRTUALLY EVERY ONE OF US AND LEADS TO OTHER, WORSE SINS IS THE BELIEF THAT THERE IS NOT ENOUGH LOVE TO GO AROUND, AND THEREFORE WHEN SOMEONE ELSE IS LOVED, HE OR SHE IS STEALING THAT LOVE FROM US.

Harold Kushner

Damned

A farm implement salesman from Motley, Minnesota left a family reunion late one nasty, frigid Sunday night in mid-March over the protests of his family. He had business up north that week and, if truth were to be told, he was glad to get away from his brothers and sisters who were always borrowing things from him. He felt like a bionic ATM or a human rent-all outlet. What added insult to injury was that they were always making sarcastic remarks about how rich he was when farmers in the area were struggling to make ends meet.

"Who needs this?" he thought. "But then, you can pick a lot of things, but not your own family!" When he got seventy miles out of town, he noticed the fuel gauge needle was rolling down toward empty. "Funny," he thought, "I'm sure I topped off the tank Saturday morning." He checked the odometer. The next town, Cushing, was at least 48 miles away. He knew that he was in the middle of farm country. With any luck, he might just get to Cushing on fumes if he slowed down.

The weatherman's voice on the radio said the temperature was thirty-five below zero and snow was expected before daybreak. It was close to midnight when he heard a thunk-thunk-thunk coming from the left front tire. He was able to slow down in time to ease the car over to the side of the road and stop it before the wheel itself was damaged. Sure enough, the tire was flat as a warm tortilla.

He bundled up, got out, walked around to the trunk, and opened it. The light was out in the trunk. It took about fifteen minutes of frantic digging to find out that the tire jack was missing too, as were his flashlight and road emergency kit.

"Damn it! That mooching brother of mine did it again! He took the car. Didn't tell me he was taking the car, and ran it 'til it was empty. I'll bet he took the tire jack and my emergency kit too!"

He started walking down the road without thinking about the temperature. The more he walked, the angrier he got. He thought about all the times his sisters and brothers took things because they were too cheap to buy them themselves. Come to think of it, their farming neighbors where they grew up did the same thing to his dad. By now his blood was up. His breathing was coming in short explosive breaths. His carotid artery was pounding. He saw a gravel road leading to a farmhouse about half a mile away. He turned up the road.

"Damned farmers, why aren't their flood lights on? They're probably so cheap they want to save a little on the electric bill and not let strangers find their way to the door when they need help," he thought. By now he was in the front yard of the farmhouse.

"They probably won't lend me tools even on a night like this!" he thought as he pounded on the front door.

The door opened and a sleep-dazed farmer was jolted awake by the sight of the salesman's red face, tight lips, and flailing arms as he shouted in the farmer's face, "You can keep your stupid jack for all I care!" With that, the salesman turned on his heel and walked back down the gravel road into the howling, icy wind.

IT'S WHEN WE GET LOST INTO [ANGER] THAT IT HURTS SOMEBODY. AND ONE WAY WE GET LOST INTO IT IS BY SAYING, "I'M NOT ANGRY!"

Stephen Levine

Keeping Up

My younger sister and I were born within a year and a half of each other. My parents planned it that way. I had three older sisters. But the gap in our ages meant that unless another child was born after me, I would be alone at home after I was seven or eight years old.

I think my younger sister came out of the womb laughing. My earliest memories of her were of her wide smile and gurgling laugh as she peered at me between the slats of her crib in our nursery. She was then, and is now, the sunshine of our lives. My mom thought it was "darling" to dress us alike. And as we went everywhere together, some people thought we were twins, except I was as dark as she was fair.

When I went to kindergarten, my world expanded beyond the nursery and backyard. I soon had a new "best friend," Jossie, and most of my time was spent with her. After all, I would always have my sister.

On the first day of summer vacation, Jossie came over to play. As I leaped out the screen door to join Jossie, my sister caught it before it slammed shut and toddled out to join us. Jossie started half skipping, half walking toward the park.

"C'mon," she yelled, as she waved toward herself. "Hurry up!"

I started to match her stride, but my sister, now right behind me, said, "Wait for me!" I waited.

Jossie ran back to my side and whispered in my ear, "Leave her. She's just a baby. She can't keep up with us!"

I felt tightness in my chest. I wanted to go with my best friend, but I didn't want to leave my sister. I didn't want Jossie to drop me as a friend because I wouldn't go along with her. So I started to speed up.

I heard a cry and looked back. My sister's face had a look of bewilderment. Suddenly she fell backward because her legs couldn't keep up with our pace. She started to cry. I felt her tears fall over my heart and tasted salt. I suddenly knew of my own desires and my power to hurt. I grew up that day in a way I would never have guessed.

I'd like to say I went back to her then and there. Neither of us remembers now. We just know that from then on she joined our games. I made sure she did. But the confident assurance that she'd always be welcome was forever shattered. Even today, the memory of that betrayal, the surprise and bewilderment in her eyes, even if it was only for a moment, still has the power to make me taste salt.

MEN BLOSSOM AND WITHER LIKE PLANTS. HEAVEN WRITES THE STORY AND ONLY THERE IS THE TRUTH KNOWN. IN THE END EACH MAN IS RESPONSIBLE ONLY FOR HIMSELF.

Isaac Bashevis Singer

WAY 3:

Positively Channel the Energy of Your Anger

I HAVE LEARNED THROUGH BITTER
EXPERIENCE
THE ONE SUPREME LESSON TO CON-
SERVE MY ANGER,
AND AS HEAT CONSERVED CAN BE
TRANSMITTED INTO ENERGY,
EVEN SO OUR ANGER CONTROLLED
CAN BE TRANSFORMED
INTO A POWER WHICH CAN CHANGE
THE WORLD.

Mahatma Gandhi

Having studied anger for many years, Hans Selye concluded that anger is a *parasympathetic response.* In other words, it's part of the "flight, fight, or paralysis" response to danger, threat, or some unpleasant event. According to Selye and contrary to popular belief, not only is anger energy, which is neutral, but it is a natural psychobiological response over which we have no domination.

Anger is God-given. God made it. God created us and we can, with the help of God, prayer, meditation, good counsel, and even medical guidance, learn ways to express our anger consistent with our unique personality, body, mind, and spirit. As Gandhi points out, we can harness the energy of anger. We can invest and transform it into a powerful conduit for the good of our families, community, work, and country. We can embrace it and turn it into power for healthy change in ourselves, to make opportunities and take responsibility for learning, growing emotionally, and deepening ourselves spiritually.

Martin Luther declared, "When I am angry, I can write, pray, and preach well for then my whole temperament is quickened, my understanding sharpened, and all mundane vexations and temptations gone."

As a graduate student at the University of Illinois, I relished whatever opportunities I had to get away to the library and to read some of the original writings of Abraham Lincoln from when he was still serving in the Illinois state legislature.

I was struck by Lincoln's methodical approach to the issue of slavery. He found it repugnant in those early years, and slowly his distaste for the brutality and inhumanity of slavery grew to an anger strong enough to motivate him to craft legislative support for abolition of slavery and emancipation of all slaves.

Similarly, Gandhi's anger at the condition of the Indian people, coupled with his belief in nonviolent action, brought an end to British imperial rule and gave birth to the nation of India. Moreover, Gandhi's model of nonviolent action in the face of oppression ignited the civil rights movement in the United States and the abolition of apartheid in South Africa.

Anger, a great motivator, can help us gather and channel the energy we need to create. Anger can compel us to compose paintings, write books, develop a city vegetable garden, or charter more effective schools for our children. Anger can be energy for great good or great evil. The choice is ours.

UNFORGIVING ANGER IS ENERGY THROWN OUT LIKE A ROPE. IT ENTANGLES ANYONE WHO GRABS ON. ANGER NEEDS TO BE ALLOWED TO TRANSFORM ITSELF INTO WHAT IT REALLY IS: A LONGING FOR UNDERSTANDING.

Christina Baldwin

Positively Channel the Energy of Your Anger

- Think about a time or two when you felt provoked by a person or event. How did you channel your anger? What action did you take? What would you do today? Re-imagine the scene, this time turning the anger-energy into a positive good.

- How can you prepare now to channel your energy in empowering ways, so that the next time you become angry, you can channel the anger-energy more positively? Should you learn judo, karate,

Aikido, or fencing? How could you channel anger so that it provides strength and protection for you?

- Meditate on these affirmations. Close your eyes and speak silently in harmony with your breathing:

  - It's okay to be angry; it's healthy to be angry.

  - I will not hurt others, or myself, or property.

  - I can find a way to channel my anger so that it works for me.

- Visualize a ring of fire, the Spirit of God, surrounding you.

- Ponder an ongoing situation in which your anger gets triggered. Spend time with each of these questions. Ideally, write responses to each one over a week's time. Leave space after each day's writing, so that you can keep adding to your reflections. At the end of the week (or longer if you aren't quite ready), take some action on your reflections:

  - Where is my anger coming from in this situation?

  - What harmful actions do I think about in this situation?

  - What are some options for action using this anger-energy to do some good? (Every day, try to brainstorm one or two positive uses of the energy.)

  - Finally, what is my action plan? What do I really choose to do with this anger-energy that will lead to good for other people and for myself?

YOU REAP WHATEVER YOU SOW. . . .
SO LET US NOT GROW WEARY IN
DOING WHAT IS RIGHT, FOR WE WILL
REAP AT HARVEST-TIME, IF WE DO
NOT GIVE UP. SO THEN, WHENEVER
WE HAVE AN OPPORTUNITY, LET US
WORK FOR THE GOOD OF ALL.

Paul of Tarsus

Ring of Fire

I had been trained to box by my father who, I think with some wisdom of experience as a brother of four sisters and as a father of only daughters, felt strongly that we needed to know how to defend ourselves physically.

I was taught how to take my power stance, take advantage of the strength in my legs, breathe from the diaphragm, bob and weave, and make a fist in a way that protected my thumbs. Learning how to throw a punch in a way that made the hardest impact was fun. I felt powerful when I did it. It was the mental attitude that was hard. I had to learn to become calm and cool.

My boxing lessons were shelved until a date-night in early spring of my senior year in college. I'd met a man, another senior from the adjoining men's college, at a "mixer" that was well chaperoned by the college staff. He asked me out to a movie the following weekend, and

I looked forward to it. In those days I was, shall we say, overly impressed by men my age that could quote lines from Heidigger and Rilke or who majored in philosophy and wrote poetry. He could and did do all of those things.

After the movie, which was forgettable, we went for a walk and ended up at his dorm house for coffee. Believe it or not, Heidigger was still the object of our conversation when suddenly his head turned toward the door and his expression went from arrogance to surprise to fear. The door swung open and three men walked in. They looked at both of us and one of them said with a leer, "Well, look what we have here! This is going to be fun."

I heard my date yell something like, "Not her. It's not what you think. She's not like the others" as he lunged for the door and stuck his foot between the doorpost and the door itself. At the same time, he was beckoning me to join him as his roommates started to slowly circle the room.

I laughed, which surprised me as it did them. I felt alert, focused, and strong. The first guy was an easy mark. I lowered my head and rammed him as hard as I could in the solar plexus.

"Ooof! What the . . . !" he cried as he collapsed to the ground, flailing his arms and gasping for air.

I had to wedge myself between my "date" and the next guy. My aim was not to inflict any more hits, but to get out. I couldn't do that because I was partially blocked. So I used the power in my legs again and rammed the steel-tipped heel of my Pappagallo pumps into the guy's foot at the top of the arch. He screamed in pain and fell back, unblocking my path. I thought about landing a blow between the bridge of his nose and his eyes just to leave a mark and make a statement.

But getting out and getting safe was smarter. I took off my shoes and started to run. I didn't know I could run so fast.

My "date" couldn't keep up with me. I heard him say, "I'm sorry, so sorry" over and over again.

"You, all of you, can go straight to hell!"

The next day he called. He and the other guys got on the line. They all called to apologize and beg me not to report them. I agreed, with some reluctance, only if they promised to stop their behavior. "And," I added, "if I ever hear of you doing anything remotely like what you tried to do to me, you'll wish you'd never seen me."

My anger built a ring of fire around me and kept me from being victimized. Despite this, there were so many more things that could have gone wrong here. And as I look back on it, from where I now stand, I'd advise a young woman in my situation to fight smart and not to go quietly. In most cases like this, it does mean going through the Dean's office or a court of law.

Paradoxically, I began to explore another question. Are there other ways to turn a threat of harm around? The question was triggered by this event and by another, four years later. This time my father intervened on my behalf with a well-established auto company when he saw that my efforts to get my "lemon" repaired were being ignored.

We drove to the company headquarters. My father went into the head office alone. Fifteen minutes later he strode out. His face was grim, his hands were clenched in hard fists. Behind him, in the doorway, stood the company's general manager. His face had a crumpled look as he slammed the door behind my father. My father got in the car, started the engine, and drove away from the parking lot.

He turned to me and said, "Why is it that we have to act like s.o.b's before we get any action these days? There's got to be another way. Anyway, take your car into them tomorrow. They're replacing the engine."

The so-called "another way" was given to me during my first summer as a law student. I was working as a law clerk for a legal aid agency. It was located on a busy corner in a changing area of Saint Paul, Minnesota. It had been the site of racial unrest in the 1960s. Small business loans and HUD monies were starting to cauterize the wounds left by rioting and residents abandoning the neighborhood.

On the corners opposite the law office were a pharmacy, a bar, and a dilapidated, vacant hotel that had seen its prime come and go. One humid July morning, I decided to get to the office early. I was excited about some research I was asked to do about a novel legal case. As I rounded the corner and approached the front door to our office, a man of about medium height lurched toward me. He said something to me, but I couldn't make it out.

Suddenly sunlight glinted off the steel blade of a knife he held in his left hand. He continued lurching forward. The mask of his face was hard, his eyes riveted on me.

I planted my feet. Hot energy leaped from my navel and spread through my chest and arms. To this day, I don't know what possessed me. Common sense would dictate that I should have taken off running. Instead, my hands opened, and I heard myself saying, "Lord, bless this good man before me!"

He stopped, literally, in his tracks. His head cocked to the left, his hands came down to his sides. He was now so close that I could smell his breath. It smelled of bourbon.

I prayed a little louder this time, "Lord, he needs your help!"

The man dropped to his knees and started sobbing. "I need help . . . Lord." I couldn't hear the rest of what he was saying. His sobs were wracking his ribs, drowning and choking off his words. By then, neighbors started to gather on the corner. They had come to catch their bus for work. One of them ran to the drugstore and called for help. Within minutes an ambulance was on the scene to whisk the man away.

That day, I continued to pray a prayer of care for him, of gratitude for care, and for the neighbors. That day I learned an answer to my father's question about how to "turn things around without being an s.o.b." I learned another way to channel the energy of anger and fear, not with my fists, but with the energy of a sound mind and the Spirit of Love.

THERE IS A VITALITY, A LIFE FORCE, A QUICKENING THAT IS TRANSLATED THROUGH YOU INTO ACTION, AND BECAUSE THERE IS ONLY ONE OF YOU IN ALL TIME, THIS EXPRESSION IS UNIQUE. IF YOU BLOCK IT, IT WILL NEVER EXIST THROUGH ANY OTHER MEDIUM. IT WILL BE LOST. . . . IT IS YOUR BUSINESS TO KEEP IT YOURS CLEARLY AND DIRECTLY, TO KEEP THE CHANNEL OPEN.

Martha Graham

Shabbat Shalom

This story is true except for the names, which have been changed at the request of the "Tenzers." Turning our anger to good teaches our children to do the same.

Otto Tenzer stepped briskly off the bottom stair of the metro transit bus and loped up the sidewalk. He was delayed at work and had to take a later bus, but if he kept this pace, he'd make it home just before sunset.

As he reached the corner of their block, he heard his neighbor Molly Sanfield call out, "Shabbat Shalom!" Just as Otto returned her blessing for a peaceful Sabbath, he heard another voice carrying through the late afternoon twilight. "You did what?" The voice was unmistakably Esther's.

Esther Tenzer, his wife of thirty-two years, was speaking to someone so loudly he could hear her at Sanfield's house more than halfway down the block. Esther, from the day Otto met her, was as gentle and dignified as she was beautiful. And she was a scholar. If she ever raised her voice, it was serious business. When Esther spoke, everyone stopped to listen. She didn't have to raise her voice to get attention. So, something was clearly wrong.

Otto leapt up the stairs to their house two at a time. He was breathless as he walked into the kitchen where Esther was standing, her face hard as marble, listening to whomever was on the phone.

"Who is it?" Otto whispered. Her lips formed the shape for "Aaron," and pointed to a letter on the kitchen table. The return address on the envelope bore the embossed seal of Aaron's college. Aaron was their youngest child. He was, as far as they knew, still in

Maine. He'd gone there as a camp counselor for the summer after his college term ended in May. The plan was that he would come home for the summer before returning to resume his expensive education.

Esther raised her voice again, "You will write Dean Cobb. You will personally make an appointment to see him before you come home. You will personally apologize to him and your professor and face the consequences.

"Or," she said, as her voice seemed to drop an octave, "I will come out there and personally shoot your other arm off!"

Otto tried not to laugh. Esther was really upset, and he didn't want to even look like he was trivializing her anger. But the visible anger of his tenderhearted partner—who couldn't even bear to step on a spider, let alone load a shotgun—amused him.

By that point, Otto began to read the letter from Dean Robert Cobb:

Dear Mr. and Mrs. Tenzer,

I was distressed to learn of the terrible accident that cost your son Aaron the use of his right hand. Fortunately, Portland has excellent orthopedic surgeons and from what I'm told, the medical care there is superb. While this comes as a shock to all of us, I trust the physical therapy Aaron is receiving will equip him for a resumption of his studies in the fall term. I have asked Professor White, our visiting professor, to extend the time for completion of his work in Biology 132 until December. If there is anything more we can do at this time, please feel free to contact me.

Sincerely,
Dean Cobb

Esther motioned for Otto to take the phone. Otto noticed tears flowing down her cheeks. "Are we having some problems, son?" he asked.

"Problems!" Esther huffed in exasperation and sat down hard. She thought Otto was always too easy on all their kids, but he was especially soft on Aaron, the youngest. She worried about how they could grow up as honorable, contributing, observant, mature men and women in this country where every allure of money, drugs, and quick fame was thrown at them. But Otto always said, "I admire young people today. I think they're figuring it out and doing just fine, better than I would have done under the same circumstances!"

Now this! Their own son! They had always taught all the children to tell the truth. "You will be able to live with the security of knowing that you are true to yourself," they would say. They wanted their children to know that they could avoid the pain of the burden of lies and cover-ups that dog our heels after lying.

Esther looked at Otto who was listening to Aaron's voice. His face was impassive. Aaron was telling him, as he had told his mother, that he couldn't finish a final project in Biology 132 before he had to leave for Bangor, Maine, and his summer job. So he left. He decided he'd figure out what to do later. What he hadn't banked on was that his biology professor left on sabbatical to a remote area of the Amazon immediately after the last class. So there was no way to arrange for an incomplete grade and a "make-up" assignment. To make things more complicated for Aaron, his matriculation was taking on a checkered pattern.

The courses Aaron loved, he aced. The ones he hated, he flunked. All of which meant that when his grade point was averaged, he needed a grade in biology to maintain probationary status and not be dismissed from college altogether. In desperation, Aaron wrote a letter to the dean of students, Robert Cobb. In the letter, he apologized for not writing sooner, but that a horrible accident had happened during his orientation weekend at the Bangor Summer Camp. A farmer, thinking Aaron was a rogue moose bothering his cattle, loaded a 12-gauge shotgun and fired it at Aaron. The shot blasted his right arm off.

Now, in August, after surgery and many weeks of rehabilitation, Aaron was writing to ask to be readmitted in September and be allowed to complete his biology project.

Otto listened to Aaron's story. Aaron finished by saying, "Dad, I want to come home."

Otto swallowed hard. "As your mother said, son."

"But Dad," Aaron wailed.

"No buts, Aaron."

"But Dad, I don't have the money to buy an extra ticket to fly to the college, then come home, then go out there again."

"Son," Otto said, "I'll arrange to have the ticket ready for you at the airport. You can work the fare off and pay me back later. Write your letter tonight, make an appointment with Dean Cobb, have your meeting with him, and then come home. We will always be here for you. Always. But, before you come home, you've got to tell Dean Cobb the truth. You need to go through this thing. We trust you to do it."

Aaron hung up the phone and started to write the letter to the Dean. As he wrote, tears fell on the paper. His were tears of embarrassment and guilt, to be sure, but also gratitude. He was grateful to his mom whose love for and belief in him were so strong. She confronted him about his behavior, not about disgrace to the family, not about past foolish things he had done, not about his character compared to his sisters and brothers, but about what he did. And gratitude for his dad's words, "We're here for you, but you've got to go through this. We know you can."

The memory sustained him as he walked into Dean Cobb's office. The Dean heard the story and accepted Aaron's apology on the spot. As for his return to school, the Dean met with a committee, which recommended Aaron return on probationary status if, but only if, Aaron finished the Biology 132 project successfully and saw the college psychologist for an evaluation.

Aaron did both. He finished the project and got a B- from the visiting professor. For his part, the psychologist, when he heard Aaron's story, laughed out loud. He wrote a letter to Dean Cobb and copied it to Aaron and his parents.

The letter was short and direct: "As to his emotional stability, I find Aaron to be absolutely sane."

Aaron wanted to frame the letter. "I'm probably the only certifiably sane student at the college," he crowed.

"Just consider yourself lucky!" replied his mother.

Years later, after Aaron was honored for his innovations and many community contributions, those who had first invested in his work were interviewed for a documentary on his life. Every person interviewed, with few variations, said the same thing about Aaron.

An investment banker said, "He was an unknown. His work was great. Original even. But then, so are a lot of others. The thing that made me want to work with him was his absolute honesty and complete lack of ego. It was refreshing."

Another said, "For him, I'd work for free. There are a lot of geniuses in this field, but he has what so many of them don't have—openness, candor, and integrity that you just don't find these days."

Esther and Otto were still alive to watch the documentary the morning it first aired, right after their morning prayer. The Creator had been good to them, but especially to Aaron whose disappointment and anger from his college years had turned to wise and caring love.

MAKE USE OF THE CREATIVE DIMEN-
SIONS THAT CAN BE RELEASED IN
ANGER. . . . THE ENERGY THAT RAGE
DEMANDS CAN SURELY BE PUT TO
BETTER USE.

Elizabeth Dreyer

Name the Wrong and Blame the Wrongdoer

THE BEGINNING OF WISDOM IS TO
CALL THINGS BY THEIR RIGHT
NAMES.

Chinese Proverb

The act of naming is powerful. Think of the care a mother and father take in choosing the name of their child. The name connotes a tie to an ancestor or a characteristic they want to entrust to their precious newborn. Similarly, the power of naming—identifying, singling out an action, a person, or a wound inflicted on us—also brings clarity. No longer is the hurt diffuse and confused. When you can name it, you can treat it.

The need for naming a wrong reminds me of the story of a man who hobbled into a doctor's waiting room. He was hunched over, his mouth in a grimace of pain as he eased himself into a chair. Another patient waiting next to him asked kindly, "Oh, dear, scoliosis and arthritis?"

"No," said the afflicted man, "do-it-yourself with cinder blocks!"

We can't get to the release of anger until we name what we are angry about. Like a surgeon wielding a laser under a scope, we can target the tumor, excise it, test it for any spread (attachments), destroy it, and begin the process of healing. However, Louis Smedes cautions us that just as surgery is not the approach of choice for every medical problem, forgiveness is not always the cure for anger. "There are wounds for which forgiving is precisely the wrong remedy."

Smedes goes on to point out that forgiving everything—even everything we can name—dilutes its meaning. "Scatter-shot forgiving," Smedes says, "is wasted forgiving." "Forgiving all," theologian Dietrich Bonhoeffer warns us, is "cheap grace." It is passive and inauthentic. Furthermore, the other person may not even know or care about what you are doing. All the while the impression of the offense is being stockpiled in our bodies ready to explode (or implode) in the future.

Like many women, I certainly have the tendency to look within when someone close to me—a colleague, family member, or a friend—does something to seriously hurt me. I think that I must have done something wrong, or even if I didn't, there must be something I could have done to prevent this from happening. Some men I know have an easier time targeting the blame when they are hurt. In some form or another most women and men struggle with the act of blaming. They rationalize with statements like,

- "She couldn't have been in her right mind."
- "He wasn't himself."
- "She was just joking and didn't mean it."

In my experience, this impulse to self-examine and analyze was further burdened by a lesson taught to me of "imagining what it was like to walk a mile in the other person's moccasins." To understand what the other person was going through was, I think, a misguided exercise in compassion. It had the effect of excusing the behavior, confusing me, and pulling the rug out from my own integrity. It did nothing to salve the pain I had to bear. Furthermore, my anger was only refueled if I found out later that my imagined rationale for the other's hurtful behavior was off the mark, and she or he intended to hurt, knew what they were doing, and reveled in the aftermath.

Wrongs done need to be named and blame needs to be appropriately placed. People do evil things that hurt us and the ones we love. Rationalizing—explaining away the wrong done and denying that anything happened—ends up just putting a lid on our hurt. The buried pain and anger fester and rot unless we can pull them out, name them, and blame the person for the wrong. Then we can choose to forgive or not and let go.

Sometimes the emperor really has no clothes: "He or she is just plain mean!" Seeing wrongs that really exist and holding the right parties responsible are not hard-heartedness and lack of charity. They are honesty and the beginnings of forgiveness.

WHEN WE DON'T BLAME HIM, WE DON'T FORGIVE HIM.

Louis Smedes

Name the Wrong and Blame the Wrongdoer

* See whether you have fallen into any of these traps that Louis Smedes outlines when you have been hurt by another:
  * *Who am I to judge?* Have you ever tried to excuse a wrong done to you or a loved one by not assigning responsibility to them?
  * *We must all share the blame.* Have you let someone off the hook because other people had a hand in the wrongdoing?
  * *We can't blame until we understand why.* If we wait to let go of anger until we understand fully why someone did an evil act, we'll be waiting until the end of time. Have you ever gotten caught in this trap?
  * *They're just victims themselves.* Have you ever used this excuse?
* Think of something that makes you angry, upset, or scared. Name the wrong and write it out in descriptive language. Then, place blame. You can place blame justly by answering "yes" to these questions:
  * Did the person actually do the wrong?
  * Did the person mean to do it?
  * Did the person choose to do it?

  For each "yes" answer write out your statement of accusation, blaming her or him for what they did. Imagine it as a bill of indictment.
* Use a large pillow to represent the person you're angry with. Find a safe, private place for you and the pillow. Sit the pillow in a chair facing you. Then

release yourself of all censorship and tell this "person" how you feel about what they've done. Read your bill of indictment. Release the energy of your anger. Don't hold your feelings back. Finally, take stock of your anger. If it isn't out yet, take a breather, and offer your indictment again until you feel release.

* Sit with your eyes closed, hands resting on your lap. Take some deep breaths. Then imagine that you're letting your anger flow out of the soles of your feet, sending it to the volcanic center of the earth where it's going to be transformed into the molten core of the planet. Name the wrong done to you; place responsibility on the person who did it. Then let the earth absorb your anger.

FORGIVENESS PRESUPPOSES REMEMBERING.

Paul Tillich

What Mysterious Lessons

Sitting in the circle of the support group, Anne was listening to each member talk about his or her experiences and steps to recovery. The chairs were arranged in a circle. Folding chairs. Stuffed chairs. Maybe it was the sofa where the occupants sank into its cushions that made the plain room somewhat homey. The members of

the group were both professionals and folks who probably didn't have as much. What they had in common
was that all were at the meeting hoping for support in
changing their lives. When Laura began to speak, Anne
could see she was trembling and almost in tears.

"I know I must offend people, but I can't let
strangers touch me. So if I don't hug you or even shake
your hand, I'm sorry. I just can't turn this over. I don't
understand what lesson God is trying to teach me. I'm
just not getting it."

Laura was a beautiful woman with a full, expressive
face and long, wavy, dark hair. Her deep brown eyes
filled with tears as she wondered several times over
what mysterious lesson there was in all of this. It had
been six months since she was assaulted. She had been
doing wonderfully at the time—six months of
sobriety—but she did take a drink the night of the
attack.

Laura now seemed to be paralyzed by fear, couldn't
work, and was on disability. This upset her because she
had always paid her own way. She never had to rely on
anyone before the assault. Now she needed people to
drive her around and even go to the store with her. What
was God thinking when he allowed this to happen?

While Laura was talking, Anne reflected that she
had heard many people around the table say something
to the effect that "everything happens for a reason."
Anne herself, at one time, had anguished because she
couldn't understand the reason God would inflict mental illness on her dad. But Anne had grown to firmly
believe that God isn't up there with a clipboard plan-
ning attacks so we learn a lesson.

However, if the rape was part of God's great plan for
her, Laura wasn't getting it, and this caused her even

more anguish. What was the lesson she was supposed to get from this? To always be afraid?

After the meeting was over and most of the people had left, Anne went to talk with Laura. She had never met her before and was not sure how Laura would react to what she had to say. But Anne felt strongly that this notion of God making bad things happen to teach people lessons was completely wrong. Her God didn't do such things, and she ached when Laura asked why she was being punished.

Anne approached Laura. "You don't know me, Laura, but I just have to respond to your words about God doing this horrible thing to you. God didn't do this to you to teach you a lesson. God didn't do this to you at all."

She continued more gently. "You were attacked because there's an evil man out there who needed to overpower a woman. You happened to be that woman. And it's not because you brought it on or you deserved it either. The man did it because he was evil. And these kinds of things happen because bad people choose to do bad things. But good people do good things. I think the lesson is to understand that God loves us and gives us our friends and other supports to help us through such horrible situations."

Laura's face slowly brightened.

"You know, no one has said that to me. That's so right."

Anne and Laura continued to talk about placing the responsibility on the person who hurt her. God wasn't responsible, nor was Laura.

Over the weeks, Anne would see Laura periodically. She seemed happier and expressed to Anne that she was less afraid. She wanted the man prosecuted and was still enraged at what he did. But she no longer questioned God's intention to teach her a lesson. And, maybe most marvelous of all, Laura started to hug again.

WHEN OUR HAND IS CLOSED IN A FIST, WE CANNOT HOLD ANYTHING BUT OUR BITTERNESS. WHEN WE DO THIS, WE STARVE OUR STOMACHS AND OUR SOULS. OUR ANGER BRINGS FAMINE ON OURSELVES.

Noah ben Shea

Ministering

A minister friend of mine, Sandra, describes the power of naming and blaming on the road to letting go of anger.

When we got married, I thought this was going to be a blessed partnership. At first it was. We were both ministers of the gospel. We seemed to complement each other. Life was full, and we soon had a growing congregation. As married ministers, we seemed to make a great team.

But after the children were born, we struggled with our relationship. He began to be jealous of my talents. So to keep things harmonious, I withdrew from my ministry. I figured I should put all my efforts into saving our marriage.

Unfortunately, the efforts were fruitless. One day while lecturing me about how to manage the house, he just snapped! He began to strike me. He only stopped when I lay limp.

He called my mother, got me help, and vowed to live separately. That didn't work. We lost the house. He began stalking me. I was never angrier. I suddenly realized I had not only been robbed of my self-esteem, but also of the gifts for creativity and joy that I always had. Now I was scrambling to live and keep my kids alive. That anger helped me look for new ways to cope. I didn't have to put up with his abuse, and I wouldn't.

He asked me to forgive him, and I agreed. But I didn't really forgive him. Not deep in my heart. Every time I took the kids on a visitation, I worried. I was scared of him, and I revisited the emotional and physical beatings. And I'd get angry all over again. Part of me said to myself, "You should have been kinder and given in more. He's been hurt too. You're a minister of the gospel after all." My insides were at war.

Eventually my kids starting getting worried because they didn't want to be near their father. After they came home from one visit, I went to tuck in the little one. She had herself turned to face the wall and wouldn't look at me. I asked her what was the matter.

She rolled over. Tears ran down her little face. She was sobbing so hard that I could hardly understand her. Finally, I heard what she said. "Mama, I'm afraid of Daddy. He seems so mad. Will he hit you again, Mama?"

Well, I started crying too. I had to do something. I tried to reassure her. But I knew that the longer I held out some kind of hope that he would change, that he wasn't really to blame, and that it would all be okay, the longer my kids and I would be afraid. I had to get on with life.

I finally just said, "I can't do this. You, God, will have to take it. Help me!" That was a real prayer.

And God has given me help, especially the strength to face my ex-husband and hold him accountable for his behavior. I'm not letting him off anymore. He had no right to hit and assault me. God's helped me see that I can still be kind and forgiving without being a victim.

The divorce is final. I'm slowly getting free of my anger. And I'm surprised, but when I think about him now, I know I'm moving more to forgiveness.

ANGER IS A TOOL FOR CHANGE WHEN IT CHALLENGES US TO BECOME MORE OF AN EXPERT ON THE SELF AND LESS OF AN EXPERT ON OTHERS.

Harriet Goldhor Lerner

Choose to Let Go of Revenge

You CAN KEEP YOUR ANGER AND
GIVE UP INNER PEACE.
OR YOU CAN LET GO OF ANGER AND
HEAL YOUR WOUNDS AT LAST.

Sidney Simon and Suzanne Simon

Contemplative monk Thomas Merton tells this story about surrendering our right to get even and letting go of our anger:

> One of the brothers had been insulted by another, and he wanted to take revenge. He came to Abbot Sisoes and told him what had taken place, saying: "I am going to get even, Father." But the elder besought him to leave the affair in the hands of God. "No," said the brother, "I will not give up until I have made that fellow pay for what he said." Then the elder stood up and began to pray in these terms: "O God, Thou art no longer necessary to us, and we no longer need Thee to take care of us since, as this brother says, we both can

and will avenge ourselves." At this the brother promised to give up his idea of revenge.

Most of us have had the experience of feeling that
we want the perpetrator to hurt as badly as we do. We
want to set up the terms and conditions of judgment
and restitution. In the heat of the moment, we want the
person banished to a place of torment. We want the law
to address our need for restitution, reformation, and
punishment. However, to paraphrase Mahatma
Gandhi, if "an eye for an eye and a tooth for a tooth"
were really meted out, "we would all of us be blind and
toothless."

It is human to keep an eye on the judge and jury in
a criminal or civil trial. If the outcome is fair, that is, it
goes the way we would have it go, we are satisfied. If it
doesn't, we look for appeal. It is "our right" to do it.
Our "right" to avenge the wrong done to us.

This isn't a plea for abolition of our justice system.
On the contrary, the "system of law, not of men"
grounded as ours is on the Mosaic Code—the Ten
Commandments—has brought civil order and balance
without which our lives would be in utter chaos.
Frontier justice and lynch mobs would rule the day.

However, we must take a hard look at the "right of
revenge" when we are hurt. To return hatred with hate,
to inflict pain with equal pain are impulses the
psalmists of old would understand. The psalmists, who
were intimate with God, made no bones about telling
God how they felt about the person or tribe that hurt
them and what they wanted God to do about it. As anyone who has turned to the psalms when in pain can
attest, they are cathartic expressions of hurt and a
demand for vengeance. Psalm 55 says, for example, "let
death come upon them . . . for evil is in their homes and
in their hearts."

The sacred psalms served a necessary function in leading to mercy. The one praying the psalms released the anger and bitterness in words, so that they did not have to act out the feelings of revenge. After all, once we have cried for revenge until we're hoarse and wept until our tears soak the ground, what then? A friend of mine once told me,

> After I had raged and cried out in all the psalms of lamentation, I said, "If I were God, this is what would happen to my enemy." I paraphrased the psalms and cried out, "Where are you? Are you impotent; are you deaf? Why won't you show me you exist?" After I got good counseling and testified at a trial and wept bitter tears, I had nothing to do but wait for God. And so I waited. First a calm came. Then an awareness that I could not know the mind of God. Then I looked for the mind of God in the words "Vengeance is mine, says the Lord" (Romans 12:19). This passage said to me "I, the Lord, get to play that part. You don't have to do it." It was freeing. I didn't have to carry out plans for revenge or getting even. For some reason I felt like I didn't have to worry about someone else's bad behavior. Just be concerned about how I was going to nullify the bad behavior by looking after the good I could do. Then one more thing hit me. How I could, if I didn't watch it, become just like my enemy, and how much I needed all the mercy and love of God for healing. Forgiveness rose up before me as a way to heal.

In a similar way, the philosopher Simone Weil once reflected on the logical consequences of revenge when she observed, "Whenever I act, it sets up a chain of

consequences, which inevitably involve a loss to someone else. So the other person learns to defend herself. I
am hurt, so I will hurt someone else. The abused
becomes the abuser. . . ." Revenge only leads to
more violence and hate, and the cycle of destruction
continues.

The suffering doesn't stop unless, with the help of
God, we choose to surrender our right for revenge.

AND FORGIVE US OUR TRESPASSES,
AS WE FORGIVE THOSE WHO TRES-
PASS AGAINST US. LOOSE THE CORDS
OF MISTAKES BINDING US, AS WE
RELEASE THE STRANDS WE HOLD OF
OTHERS' GUILT. LIGHTEN OUR LOAD
OF SECRET DEBTS AS WE RELIEVE
OTHERS OF THEIR NEED TO REPAY.
FORGIVE OUR HIDDEN PAST, THEIR
SECRET SHAMES, AS WE CONSISTENT-
LY FORGIVE WHAT OTHERS HIDE.

Neil Douglas-Klotz

Choose to Let Go of Revenge

- Spend a few minutes recalling an event in which
  you were hurt or betrayed or deeply disappointed.
  Then, in your own words, write to the Holy One
  about your anger, resentment, rage, or hurt. Express

all your feelings of revenge. Then end your writing by inviting the Holy One to be the judge and jury. Surrender your right of retribution to the Creator of the universe.

- Find a psalm from the Bible or other sacred book, or passage from literature that expresses your outrage and desire for revenge. Read the passage, meditate on it, and proclaim it out loud. Then write your own version of it. End by offering it to the Holy One.

- Bring two small tables to a quiet corner of your home. If you wish, place a picture or drawing of your enemy on one table and a picture of yourself on the other. Place a braided cord on each table. On scraps of paper write regarding this relationship:

  - things you've done in the past that you regret,

  - anything you might have said or done to harm this person,

  - debts you would repay if possible,

  - pledges or promises made that you didn't keep,

  - expectations you've had for this relationship that didn't work out for you.

  On other scraps of paper, write:

  - mistakes the other person made that caused pain or difficulty for you,

  - anything the other person did or said to harm you,

  - debts the person owes,

  - pledges or promises the other person made, but didn't keep,

  - expectations of the person or dreams shared with that person that didn't work out.

As you take a scrap of paper for yourself, burn the debt, or mistake, or regret, or expectation in a fire-proof container. After you have burned the scrap, loosen a strand from the cord on your table. Repeat this action at the table of the enemy. As you complete this action, pray or say the Aramaic prayer of forgiveness,

> And forgive us our trespasses, as we forgive those who trespass against us. Loose the cords of mistakes binding us, as we release the strands we hold of others' guilt. Lighten our load of secret debts as we relieve others of their need to repay. Forgive our hidden past, their secret shames, as we consistently forgive what others hide.

This ritual can be repeated as often as you wish, whenever you wish, until the cord is nothing but strands of thread. You might want to hang the thread outside in early spring so returning migratory birds can make their nests with it.

- Sit or lie in a comfortable position. Relax completely, let all tension drain out of your body. Breathe deeply and slowly. Visualize the light of God radiating through your heart; feel the warmth and life of God coursing through your veins, flushing out all toxins. Say clearly in harmony with your breathing, "Nothing separates me from the love of God."

- Imagine that you are placing someone who hurt you in a pink bubble of compassion and floating them into the care of our Creator. This is about blessing them and letting them go. Remember that you are doing this for yourself! Even after doing this release work, it is not uncommon for the hurtful one to come into our minds occasionally. If so, just put them back into that pink bubble of compassion and send them off. An effective affirmation to accompany this sending off goes like this: "I set you free to live your life as I free myself to live my life."

HATING PEOPLE IS LIKE BURNING
DOWN YOUR OWN HOUSE TO GET
RID OF A RAT.

Harry Emerson Fosdick

The Supreme Virtue

Well over a decade ago, a scholar of Jewish mysticism told me a story that directly addresses the question about letting go of revenge. It has stayed with me all these years.

During the holy days of the Jewish calendar—*Rosh Hashanah* ("Days of Awe") and *Yom Kippur* ("Days of Atonement")—devout Jews examine whether there is something which they have done for which they need to ask forgiveness. This festival includes an act of *teshuvah* or repentance, a letting go of resentment and the need for revenge.

Some Jewish teachers declare that during these holy days, a band of accusing angels tells God about all of a person's faults—of which naturally there are many. Another band of angels pleads the person's case before God, defending the poor sinner. If and only if these angels make their case for the defendant will the world continue to exist as it is now.

In the wisdom of the Holy One, angels who will defend human beings must pass a series of tests. After all, they need to understand what virtues to recognize in people. If they can learn to spot and evaluate those virtues, they should be able to defeat the case of the accusing angels. And so, the world will stay in existence.

Thus, one time, God told a candidate-defending angel, "I have a task for you. Name the supreme virtue that you see in humankind."

Eager to please the Holy One, the angel applied all its powers, looking for the highest virtue. At last, the angel thought that the answer had been found. In a bustling city, two men stood on a corner. The elder gentleman tottered on his feet as he attempted to pass in front of trolleys and wagons filled with goods. In the middle of the roadway he became confused and froze in place. Seeing the old man's danger, the younger man jumped from the sidewalk, bolted out into traffic and shoved the old man to safety just before the trolley would have killed him. Sadly, the selfless man was run over and killed instantly.

"Ah," said the angel, "this is the supreme virtue." The angel took a single drop of the courageous man's blood and, showing it to the Holy One, said, "I saw a selfless, caring man give up his own life's blood to save the life of a helpless stranger. I believe that this must be the supreme human virtue."

The Holy One agreed that indeed such selfless courage was an excellent virtue, but it was not the supreme human virtue. So God sent the novice angel back to earth to search again.

The angel arrived at a small village in the countryside. Here the angel heard the agonizing moans of a mother giving birth in her modest dwelling. Even with the midwife's skill and encouragement, the birth was long and painful. Finally, a wizened, wailing baby was born. When the mother took it into her arms, her face filled with joy and certain love.

"Certainly such love has to be the supreme human virtue," the angel concluded. Feeling confident now, the angel took a drop of the mother's sweat as testimony to her supreme virtue. The angel held the drop of perspiration before the Holy One as his evidence and declared, "This mother's gift of life through her agony has to be the supreme virtue."

The Compassionate One nodded and told the angel, "Certainly such sacrifice to create new life is profoundly virtuous. Out of such love the world will continue. However, even this is not the supreme virtue. Try one last time to find it."

Knowing that extreme vigilance coupled with infinite patience would be required, the angel searched everywhere, observing all possible examples of virtue among women and men. The angel searched and searched.

Late one evening, the angel spotted a man hurrying through a forest. The man's face shone with sweat. His eyes blazed, his fists clenched. The angel had never seen such fierce concentration and intense anger before. This was certainly not what the angel was looking for. Nevertheless, the angel followed.

Reviewing the man's story, the angel discovered that he had served a long sentence in prison for a crime he did not commit. While behind bars, he had sworn to get even. Having just been released, he was hurrying to exact revenge on the villain for whose crime he had suffered.

The angel observed the vengeance-crazed man stop and begin cautiously approaching a cabin. Inside the cabin was the one who had committed the crime. The hunter peeked into a window out of which glowed warm candlelight. He held still, gazing inside. Revenge was at hand.

Just as the man was raising his pistol, he heard the happy gurgling of an infant and the pleasant laughter of a woman. Through the window, he saw his enemy's wife holding a smiling infant out to the man he wanted to kill. The angel could not breathe. He knew that the couple had only been married a year and that the new-born baby daughter was the light of their lives.

Seeing the love in his enemy's face, the would-be assassin tossed down the pistol and broke into tears. He could not end such love and rob the family of their joy. Taking one last tender look, the man stole back into the woods and never returned.

"Truly, this is the supreme virtue of all that I have seen. Humans are capable of marvelous goodness, but to turn one's back on vengeance and forgive a hated enemy must be the supreme virtue!"

To this, the Holy One agreed.

TO FORBEAR MEANS TO HAVE PATIENCE, TO BEAR UP AGAINST, TO CHANNEL EMOTION. THESE ARE POWERFUL MEDICINES. . . . TO REFRAIN FROM UNNECESSARY PUN-ISHING STRENGTHENS INTEGRITY OF ACTION AND SOUL.

Clarissa Pinkola Estes

Taking Care

In the mid-1940s, my father struck out on his own to establish a road and bridge construction company. Within a decade, his company built highways and bridges that were part of the mass infrastructure connecting states and regions throughout the United States after the Second World War. My father's capital investment and income burgeoned along with the size of the company.

The company was unique, not only for its time, but for today as well. Each crewmember held stock in the company, and decisions about process were developed in teams. While there were specialists and engineers, everyone worked as a unit to get the job done well. Furthermore, my father's income never exceeded fifteen percent more than the lowest paid worker in the crew. In the early fifties, the company was poised for expansion and diversification.

However, as it happens in human enterprises, there was always room for improvement, if not disagreement and outright dissension. There was also ample opportunity for misappropriation of funds when times were prosperous. Some supportive banking friends brought their suspicions of misappropriation of company money to my father's attention. My father also became aware of dissension and jealousy among certain members of the crew toward each other. There was evidence that someone was furtively giving my father's estimates for future jobs to competitors. The situation called for objective outside analysis. The accountants confirmed the worst. Massive amounts of money had been slowly siphoned off over the years. The only way forward, they advised, was to dissolve the existing company and start all over again.

My father's integrity and talent ensured financial backing. There were those who counseled legal action as well as service club, if not church, censure. Like some of Job's counselors, they questioned my father's naive trust of others and hoped he'd be wiser the next time. My father chose a different path. He pointed out how much better it was to trust others, even if we risked betrayal, because to live cynically, sophisticated as it may seem, was really to live in fear of others. He wasn't going to live in fear of anyone.

Another difference set him apart from his critics. His priorities in setting out a strategy for dissolution were based on a business principle I'm not sure many would agree with today. Nonetheless, he consciously followed it.

He said his first responsibility as a businessman was to God. His life was in God's hands. He saw that his daily and final accounting was to God. The second responsibility was to make sure the men who worked with him as well as their families were taken care of. The third responsibility was to our family. And because these responsibilities were entrusted to the care of God, he need not worry. That's not to say he didn't worry. He did. All I'm saying is that he had a guiding principle that he believed in and adhered to especially during this arduous time in his life.

When the time came to go through the dissolution proceedings, he called the men in, explained the situation, the choices before him, including legal and tactical ones, and the package he developed for theirs and their families' care. He really was not naive. Not completely. He had expected some would deny their part in the wrongdoing or blame others. He expected anger.

But he was surprised and hurt by his young associate's reaction. The associate had been recruited as soon as he'd left the service for his quiet courage and quick intellect. My father had hoped this man would some day take over the company. However, when he discovered the associate's role in compromising the company, he felt he had no other choice but to help him secure another professional position where the young associate could excel. Yet, the associate's reaction was an angry outburst at my father, which carried beyond the office.

I think what may have hurt the most were the false accusations and misunderstanding between my father and that man. Despite this, my father never dwelled on it and always included him in his prayers.

About ten yeas later, my father received a letter from his angry, former associate. It took us all by surprise. Here is what he said:

> Despite the blows of misunderstanding and gossip, you made sure everyone was taken care of so our families would be secure. You never held anything against me; I can never thank you enough.

In my twenties then and home on school vacation, the letter took me back to another summer when I was fourteen and my bewilderment at why our family moved to the city so abruptly from the home and small town where my sister and I had spent our childhood. I was also curious about why my father restructured his business to concentrate on bridge building alone. It was never really clear to me until the associate's letter arrived.

Over the years I had learned some other details from my father's friends. That is why the associate's

letter arriving as it did all those years later was so profoundly moving. The associate was determined to set
things right again and accepted responsibility for whatever pain he had brought my father in the past.

What brought a real sense of ease between them
was his expression of gratitude. They both had prospered and were able to give a legacy of an example of
what can happen if revenge is surrendered for mercy
and forgiveness.

FORGIVENESS IS A TREMENDOUS
STRENGTH. IT IS THE ACTION OF
SOMEONE WHO REFUSES TO BE
CONSUMED BY HATRED AND
REVENGE.

Helen Prejean

Remember That Your Enemy Is Human Too

EVEN IN THE GRIMMEST TIMES IN
PRISON, WHEN MY COMRADES AND I
WERE PUSHED TO OUR LIMITS, I
WOULD SEE A GLIMMER OF HUMAN-
ITY IN ONE OF THE GUARDS, PER-
HAPS JUST FOR A SECOND, BUT IT
WAS ENOUGH TO REASSURE ME AND
KEEP ME GOING.

Nelson Mandela

Writer C. S. Lewis observed that forgiveness is not just human fairness. Forgiveness means excus-ing things that really can't be excused at all. Louis Smedes amplifies this idea further: "If we really under-stood why someone had to hurt us, we would know he could not help himself and we would excuse him instead of blame him. And if we excuse someone, we do not need to forgive him because we only forgive the ones we blame."

Forgiving the inexcusable is exceedingly hard. We don't really have to do it at all. But if we choose to take the step for our own good health, it is made easier if we can begin to understand a little, not all, about the humanity of the one who has hurt us. This seems to contradict the fallacy that "to understand all is to forgive all." On the contrary, forgiveness attempts to understand—as much as possible—the humanity of the one that injured us, not to remove responsibility for their actions.

Whenever I've tried this, it makes forgiving a little easier. It's important to proceed slowly and with gentleness toward ourselves because the hurt is, and will be for some time, raw. It's also important to confirm that the person who hurt us had a choice. They didn't have to do what they did. That is the mystery of free will. Having said this, even a little grasp of what may have influenced them when they inflicted pain or harmed us will ease our steps of forgiveness.

Theologian John Patton believes that forgiveness is a discovery that happens when we gain insight into what it means to be human. The key insight, that is at the heart of this discovery, is to recognize that we and the one who caused us shame or hurt or injury are in some ways alike and that we share a common humanity. Thus, Mother Teresa was once heard to have said, "There is a little of a Hitler in me!" That wasn't false humility on her part. It was a candid admission about our common humanity—the base as well as the noble.

When it comes down to it, we humans always disappoint. And those closest to us hurt us the most. But we hurt and disappoint them the most too. One biblical proverb says, "Don't put your faith in the princes of this world, but put your trust in the Holy One." The

Creator never wavers in supporting and loving us and is as close as our breath. Human beings—including us—inevitably hurt one another. None of us is innocent.

So here is a mystery. How do we discover the humanity of another? How do we tell others about ourselves in the most transparent way to become closer, to come to an understanding? We tell others our stories and hear others tell their stories. Nobel Peace Prize winner and author Elie Wiesel said that God created humans because God loves stories. How can we get a little insight into why someone hurt us so we can be released from the anguish of shame or hurt? By learning their stories. How can we be released from the anguish of pain we have caused others? By being able to tell another who will give us their full, respectful attention to our story. We want to be understood. Likewise understanding the story of our enemy can aid our journey to forgiveness. After all, the stories of all the great scriptures call humanity to have compassion for one another, to live in harmony, to understand their common humanity.

There's a paradox here as well. If we and others in our human family are not perfect, we hurt others and make foolish judgments that bring pain to others. Others bring us pain as well. But, we are being perfected in the image of the Creator, and that Creator is the Holy One who forgives. William Menniger describes the paradox succinctly: "Forgiveness is demanded by the very nature of man and woman. It is not only divine, it is also human. God commands it because without it we are less than human, with it we are more."

I have been taught that in the mystical tradition of Judaism, it is believed that the *Shekinah* (the Holy One's loving, gracious, and over-arching presence in the world) suffered a series of self-humiliations as the created world evolved. The Creator "suffered" in the creation of the world, in the choosing of the patriarchs, when the chosen people went into exile, when the Holy One went with the people into the *Shoah*, the Holocaust. If we follow the line of this teaching, it means that there is no human heartbreak, no betrayal, no alienation and exile that doesn't find itself in the suffering heart of the Creator. And so it will be until the end of this time. Therefore, the work of every observant Jew is one of *tikkun*, to make the broken world whole again.

This work of *tikkun*, forgiveness and co-creation, is hard. It means facing ourselves honestly and acknowledging what we've done to bring pain to others as well as suspending ill will toward our enemy and listening to his or her story.

Forgiveness *is* a paradox. In discovering and telling the truth about ourselves through our own stories, we learn to be merciful. If we are not merciful, we will end our lives. In learning to discover the truth about our enemies through listening to their stories, we will be able to take an important step to forgiveness: suspension of ill will. The payoff is a rediscovery of freedom to love ourselves and to love others as well. The healing can then begin.

WHEN YOU SEE YOUR ENEMY AND YOURSELF IN THE WEAKNESS AND SILLINESS OF THE HUMANITY YOU SHARE, YOU WILL MAKE A MIRACLE OF FORGIVING A LITTLE EASIER.

Louis Smedes

Remember That Your Enemy Is Human Too

- Imagine you have been assigned to interview your enemy for a newspaper story you are to write. Ask for the following information:
  - Where did you grow up?
  - Describe your parents, siblings, and grandparents.
  - What are your favorite hobbies?
  - What do you dream about?
  - What are your likes and dislikes?
  - Name and describe the event that brought you the most pain. What did you learn from the incident?
  - What are your worst fears?
- Take training and volunteer to care for any people who are outcasts in society. Or, simply bring food and attentive listening to places that feed and house the homeless.
- Find a smooth rock. With a marker, write the offenses of your enemy on the rock. Hold the rock in your hand tightly. Then release the rock into a forest, creek, or gravel pit and say a prayer for mercy.
- Sometimes we feel tied to the one who hurt us. It is almost as if there is an imaginary cord that links the victim and the perpetrator in a hurtful act. It can be quite freeing to cut this kind of tie that binds. To do so, enter into a quiet meditation time.

  Let yourself see the person who has harmed you and the cord that connects you. Notice where the cord is connected to your body. Now ask for a method to cut, sever, or detach the cord from your body. Ask that this method be gentle and bring no harm to you. As you cut the cord, see the person moving or floating away from you, out of your personal space. Imagine them moving as far away as you like. If you no longer want this person in your life, let them float entirely away from your sphere. Notice how you feel emotionally and in your body. Finally, place your hand over the place on your body where the cord was attached, imagine that you are filling the area with love and comfort and that the attachment site has closed and healed.

- Sit comfortably. Relax. Close your eyes. Breathe deeply. Then let your imagination take you into this meditation:

It is a sunny, warm day in August. You are at a friend's annual clambake party in her garden on a bluff overlooking a cove of the ocean in Maine. She has invited everyone you both have ever known to the party. The guest list includes your old enemies (name names). You arrive a little late, entering the garden from the porch at the back of the house. You pause at the top stair of the porch. It gives you a panoramic view of all the guests all the way out to the ocean cove. The guests are all there. Watch as they interact with each other. See if you can find at least one attractive attribute about each one including your enemies.

As you descend the stairs of the porch, your hostess runs up to greet you and says, "How wonderful, you can be the first one to ride in the hot air balloon. Please say you will; then everyone else will follow!"

As the balloon rises, you are able to see your enemies (name names) from a distance as if you were looking at them through the reverse lens of a telescope. Describe what you see. The warm rays of the sun caress your arms as you rise. Enfold the warmth of the sun in your arms and draw the warmth into your heart. Hold it there. Then take the rays of the sun in your arms again. Hold it; then release it to surround (name names) your old nemesis. Repeat the gift of the healing warmth of the sun for each member of the party. Thank the Creator and your hostess for generosity and loving-kindness.

COMPASSION IS THE AWARENESS THAT WE ARE ALL IN THE SAME BOAT AND THAT WE ALL SHALL EITHER SINK OR SWIM TOGETHER. . . . ALTHOUGH LOVING ONE'S ENEMIES REQUIRES GRACE, COMPASSION FOR ONE'S ENEMIES IS A HUMAN POSSIBILITY.

Rollo May

Our Job to Forgive

"**W**e are to live as he lived. God has forgiven us many times, so it's our job to forgive too. For our part there was no thought of hatred," explains Patricia Keane, a Catholic nun.

She explains her position so rationally, so logically that it is hard to recall that Keane, now seventy, had been seriously injured, almost killed, by a man who bludgeoned her with a two-foot statue of the Blessed Virgin holding the Christ child two years before as she prayed alone in her small convent chapel. The man had already inflicted mortal wounds on two other sisters in the convent kitchen and left another badly beaten.

Keane should have recognized the man as he stormed into the chapel. He was Mark Bechard, a thirty-eight-year-old jazz musician who had been regularly attending evening mass at the chapel for about a year. "But his eyes were so wild," she says, that "he wasn't the same person I knew." His attack on her ended abruptly when two police officers burst into the chapel with guns drawn and ordered Bechard to drop his weapon and raise his arms in surrender. He complied and was calmly led away.

This bizarre atrocity occurred on January 27, 1996, in the sleepy town of Waterville, Maine (population 17,500). Here the Servants of the Blessed Sacrament, a contemplative order of sisters, had maintained a white clapboard convent and a yellow chapel since 1947. The sisters are well respected, and townspeople have always felt free to stop at the chapel for prayers or services.

Police and emergency medical workers were deeply affected by the carnage they found that night. Sisters

Marie Julien Fortin, sixty-seven, and Edna Mary Cardozo, sixty-eight, were dead, both beaten, stabbed, and stomped on by Bechard after he broke in through the back door. Both had been especially friendly toward the somewhat eccentric Bechard in the past and had rushed forward in an attempt to try to calm him down as he entered. Sister Mary Anna DiGiacomo, sixty-two, also beaten, survived with severe injuries. Keane suffered a fractured wrist and cut hand and required multiple stitches in her face and head.

Bechard, a Waterville native, had been diagnosed in the late 1970s with bipolar disorder and schizophrenia, a potent combination, and had been admitted to Augusta Mental Health Institute for sustained treatment on ten occasions in the intervening years. People with his form of illness often hear disturbing voices and noises that can lead to unpredictable, violent outbursts. Mark Bechard had a history of such violent incidents, yet at the time he was considered sufficiently stable (with medication) to live in the outside world.

David Mizner, a writer who grew up in Waterville and resided in New York City, learned of the tragedy and returned to his hometown to see what effects it would have. "As I read about the attack, I was sure it would cause Waterville to fall apart," he wrote for an article in *Hope* magazine. "I knew enough about crime in small towns to know they don't handle brutal acts of violence well. Seldom touched by such horror, residents would react irrationally, perhaps even vengefully." But Mizner was surprised at what he found.

To be sure there was some panic. Several clients at a nearby mental health center received threatening phone calls. The attorney appointed to represent Bechard also received a death threat, lost one of her regular clients, and was shunned by the police officers who had worked with her. But the calm, prayerful reaction of the sisters, especially Keane, served to counter the hostile mood. A columnist at the local paper admitted, "I've been heavy on revenge . . . but I simply cannot see these women reacting that way. I absolutely believe those sisters are somewhere out there, very concerned that we are not going to be able to forgive their murder."

Four days after the incident, 1,000 people packed the Notre Dame Parish church a block from the convent for a public prayer service. In her eulogy, former Mayor Nancy Hill said, "I encourage us to pray that Mark's family will feel the loving support of Waterville. Let us dedicate ourselves to work so that Waterville will be a place where all who are needy have the support and love they need. Then we will have given the sisters a legacy of which they and we can be proud." Due to the extraordinary publicity about the incident, the state legislature later demanded improved oversight of mental patients living in local communities.

When she was sufficiently recovered, Keane visited Bechard's parents to pledge her prayers and assure them she harbored no hard feelings toward their son. Mark himself was found legally insane a few months after his rampage and sent to a state institution where he will remain for many years, possibly for life.

In November, ten months after the assault, police returned the badly damaged statue of Mary and the child to the sisters, who had it repaired by a local artist and returned to its appropriate pedestal in the chapel. On the first anniversary of the killings, the chapel was filled as Keane stood beside the statue and said, "Let us pray for the mentally ill, especially Mark Bechard, that they may find healing and peace."

Writer Mizner acknowledged his relief at the city's ability to cope with such a tragedy. He cited civic leaders "who strive to shape public sentiment for the better, an attorney willing to lose friends and clients to serve a man in need," and especially, "a group of women who refuse to see the memory of their friends and sisters tarnished by hate."

Keane says the ten sisters, aged fifty-eight to eighty-one, who make up the community today have more lay volunteers and more candidates for daily prayer than they ever had before. "People come in and ask us to pray for them," she says. "We do, of course. And we always pray for Mark too."

Robert McClory

THE FORGIVING STATE OF MIND IS A MAGNETIC POWER FOR ATTRACTING GOOD.

Catherine Ponder

Tikkun in Action

Mahatma Gandhi went on a long hunger strike to protest the terrible street fighting being waged between Hindus and Muslims. Gandhi's devoted followers beseeched him to end the hunger strike, but to no avail.

One day a frantic man rushed into Gandhi's bedroom, pushed Gandhi's advisors aside, and threw bread at Gandhi, shouting and imploring him to eat. He pleaded, "I'm going to hell, but not with your death on my soul!"

Gandhi replied softly, "Only God decides who goes to hell."

In despair, the man cried out, "I killed a child! I smashed his head against a wall!"

Calmly Gandhi asked, "Why?"

In a wrenching voice, his eyes welling with tears, the man confessed, "They killed my son, my boy!"

As the man held his hand parallel to his waist to show the height of a child of four or five years, he continued, "The Muslims killed my son!"

Gandhi, still in a calm, quiet voice, told him, "I know a way out of hell." The man's eyes fastened on Gandhi as Gandhi gave him an exit out of his hell.

"Find a child," Gandhi said. "A child whose mother and father have been killed. A little boy about this high." Gandhi raised his hand to the same height as the man's murdered son as he continued, "And raise him as your own."

The man's face first relaxed, then turned to astonishment as Gandhi ended with the direct order, "Only make sure that this child is a Muslim and that you raise him as one."

FORGIVENESS IS THE FINAL FORM OF
LOVE.

Reinhold Niebuhr

For Your Own Good, Decide to Forgive

THERE IS A HARD LAW . . . THAT
WHEN A DEEP INJURY IS DONE TO
US, WE NEVER RECOVER UNTIL WE
FORGIVE.

Alan Paton

Our bodies are the repositories of memory. Fortunately, memory is selective. Otherwise our bodies would explode from the sheer accumulation of the sum of our experience. In any case, why then does the memory select what it does? Why does it continuously catalogue our wrongs until the collection becomes a grudge, eating away at our peace of mind and capturing our attention—even in our dreams?

Surely this hanging on to bitterness and anger has to do with the depth of hurt that has been inflicted on us or on those we care about. It has to do with immediacy and intimacy. Writer Thomas Keating concludes that it also has to do with the threats to our self-esteem, our desire for control, or our security.

When we sense a negative memory slithering out of our memory to ensnare us in feelings of resentment, bitterness, or jealousy, we may select one of these approaches:

• nurse it, tucking it away in our grudge bag to lug around on our backs;

• throw it at someone else and duck if it boomerangs back on us;

• tell it, like a frisky dog, to "get down, Fido!" and then stuff it inside until it leaks out and poisons our heart and corrodes our stomach.

But, there are other ways. We can tell it to a trusted counselor or spiritual advisor. We can let go of our attachment to it. We can meditate. In meditation, whenever the negative memory floats by, we can wave at it and say, "Thanks for sharing!" And, we can, with strong trail guides, plot the map for a journey of forgiveness and freedom.

And despite all that we have heard so often, we must remember: Forgiveness is for our good. If it helps the other person—fine. But first and foremost, forgiveness heals us. And we must heal ourselves first.

There is an apocryphal Hasidic story I once heard about the angel of forgetfulness and a Rabbi who had a memory so accurate that he called it a curse. The Rabbi's memory was so prodigious, he could look at the page of a scroll and recite every word from memory.

This memory was a useful gift to be sure, but it spread out to everything. For example, the Rabbi remembered every detail about a person: the person's ancestors, actual events in their lives, and the date, time, and season something occurred. His memory was a marvel to those who forgot where they put their keys in the morning, let alone when an important event might have happened. But for the Rabbi, who remembered every vulgar detail as well as every noble deed a person did, it was a deeply distressing burden.

As the years went on, the Rabbi's face became more furrowed and his posture became more stooped, as if he were carrying a heavy sack of bricks on his back. People worried because the light in his eyes became dim and he seemed more and more preoccupied. For his part, the Rabbi felt as if the memory of bad things people did was oozing into his stomach and poisoning everything he digested. So he prayed to Adonai, the Holy One, for help.

And, Adonai mercifully sent an angel of forgetfulness to visit the Rabbi as he slept. The angel anointed the Rabbi's head with warm, sweet oil as a seal to wipe away the burden of memory of the wicked things people do.

In the morning, when the Rabbi went to *schul*, everyone was amazed to see him striding briskly and light-footed down the street. His head was erect. His face was radiant and his eyes were once again clear, cornflower blue. As he happily greeted everyone, an unmistakable fragrance of sweet oil wafted around them. The Rabbi entered the synagogue and opened the Torah and remembered, as he recited from the text of Exodus 34, the attributes of God are to act with patience, mercy, love, kindness, grace, and compassion. And this is what he did remember forevermore.

Just as with the Rabbi in the apocryphal tale, the constant memory of pain or hurt caused by someone else can rob us of peace and health that comes with forgiving others. To forgive means to give up resentment, to remit or pardon another for what they have done wrong. It is a gift of freedom and peace that we can give ourselves—not just to the other person. It is for our good health and ability to go on with our lives. Most important, it frees our hearts for giving and receiving the love we so very much deserve.

We've all met persons who clutch on to every ugly thing that happened in their lives. They worry over past wrongs like a six-year-old massaging her loose tooth over and over again with her tongue. Nostrils flair, mouths become pinched, and the chest heaves as persons of this kind get ready to blast the story of who, how, and why they were wronged. In time, these constant tales of woe drive friends and family away. The sour bitterness leaks out of every pore, polluting the air between them and any that would care for them.

Letting go of the resentment and constant mulling over of the wrong does not mean that we forget, as in "forgive and forget." No. We must learn from these wrongs for our own good. If we've been naïve and suffered the consequences, we don't want to allow a repeat of the wrong. However, staying stuck in memories of old wrongs is like being locked in solitary confinement.

The key that unlocks the prison is forgiveness, letting go of the attachments that bind us to the person who has wronged us or to the event itself. Forgiveness is an act of conscious awareness that we are releasing that person or debt and freeing ourselves to live in the present moment. Forgiveness allows our memories to be free so that life can flow in us again.

FATHER POEMEN SAID TO FATHER
ISAAC, "LET GO OF A SMALL PART OF
YOUR RIGHTEOUSNESS, AND IN A
FEW DAYS YOU WILL BE AT PEACE."

Saying of the Desert Fathers

For Your Own Good, Decide to Forgive

- Review the past twenty-four hours. Write about an incident or a memory in which you revisited a negative memory that triggered resentment in you. Describe how intense it was on a scale of one to five. Try to write a description of where in your body you felt the anger. What did you do with it? How would you describe your acceptance of your behavior: Were you pleased with it? Neutral? Or is there something you'd like to do differently?

- Find a clear bowl. Fill it with pure, warm water. For some moments, breathe slowly and deeply. Then, imagine that you are grounding your feet to the earth with a cord of silver. Say a prayer for yourself and the person with whom you are angry.

  Cup your hands around the place where you feel the anger, name it, and draw it out. Then, place your cupped hands into the bowl, hold the water, and then open your fingers, releasing the water. As you do so, name the memory of hurt, anger, or resentment that you are releasing. Let the water take them away, purifying your spirit. Wash your hands as many times as you need to forgive and let go.

When you have finished the washing, just sit quietly and bring to mind all for which you are grateful. Offer thanks for the goodness that you embrace and that has embraced you.

- Do this imagination exercise. Imagine you are in a forest of cedars; the scent of cedar boughs and soft, warm breezes surround you. All is still except for the song of a cedar waxwing. You have placed your anger in a nest of sage. The nest slowly catches fire as you place it gently in a small boat made of cedar boughs. The fragrance of sage rises as you lower the boat into a rivulet running from a cedar spring before you. You release the boat and, as it floats away, your anger smolders and is slowly quenched by the water from the cedar spring that bears it away.

- Sit in a comfortable, quiet place. Take a few deep breaths to relax your body and bring calm to your mind. If a negative image comes to your mind, greet it, breathe it, permit yourself to feel it, and then watch it glide away. Or you might wave at it and say, "Thank you for sharing!"

YOU CANNOT PREVENT THE BIRDS OF SORROW FROM FLYING OVER YOUR HEAD, BUT YOU CAN PREVENT THEM FROM BUILDING NESTS IN YOUR HAIR.

Chinese proverb

A Living Memorial

During a recent spring, I was in Atlanta to address a convention of graduate educators. During some free time before the conference dinner, I took the opportunity to make a pilgrimage to the Ebeneezer Baptist Church where Dr. Martin Luther King, Jr., was reared, had his first call, and where his funeral was held after his assassination. The memorial to Dr. King and the civil rights movement, located across the street, is majestic in its unadorned simplicity. I was drawn there in large part to honor Dr. King, but also to relive a time of change when justice actually did roll down like water to forever alter the land on which I stood.

As I walked through the museum, my stomach clutched as I saw pictures of state troopers with bayonets and cattle prods descending on and beating young African-Americans who had peacefully assembled in front of a church. There were other scenes of water cannons and attack dogs being turned on civilians—both black and white. I felt sick. The sounds and images long ago etched in my memory leapt in front of me.

I exited into a soft late afternoon light, crossed the street, and waited in front of the Ebeneezer Baptist Church to catch a bus back to my hotel. A National Park Ranger, a fit, willowy young woman with a face of chiseled ebony, closed one of the doors of the church to signal that it was almost closing time. We fell into a conversation about what the impressions were of those who come to visit. She asked what my feelings were about the memorial, and I told her how profoundly moving it was and how hard it was reliving those times.

"There are so many who come out reliving their anger and bitterness," she remarked. "We really need to release that and go on!"

I objected that even if we've gone on with life, the body stores that horrible memory and letting go is easier said than done.

"But," she said with the lovely assurance of youth, "bitterness and seething hatred doesn't honor memory. It won't build a just community!"

My bus arrived, and I had to end the conversation. As I turned to say goodbye, I took a last look at the young woman. In my sight was a spiritual heir of Dr. King. In her willingness to forgive, she is well on her way to building what Dr. King envisioned as "The Beloved Community."

To forgive is the best form of self-interest, because I'm also releasing myself from the bonds that hold me captive.

Desmond Tutu

Honoring the Coyote

A Native-American tribal interpreter told this story to me. I promised that I would honor his request that neither he nor his tribe be identified. "Honoring the Coyote" describes a sacred practice for claiming and embracing the anger that poisons us. Here is his story:

When I was forty years old, I returned home to the reservation, to the place of my birth, an old log cabin that my mother and father had built. It was not large, just fifteen by twenty-two feet, nor was it in good condition. The door was off the hinges and there were holes chopped in the floor by an ax where some squatters had cut wood to feed the wood stove. The caulking had fallen out from between the logs, and the cool spring prairie wind blew through.

I had been unable to keep a job for any length of time, even though I had gone through college on the G. I. Bill, was qualified as a teacher, and was a good worker. I had lost my family of eighteen years. My wife divorced me and took our seven children with her. The automotive dealership was after me to repossess my car, and I had outstanding checks here and there. Even a friend who had once helped me refused to bail me out again. I was alone, penniless, and dispirited. I was addicted to alcohol. I pulled up the last thing on the property worth anything, the red outside water pump, and hocked it for a case of beer. I did not know how I would go on.

I felt that if I did not get a drink, I would die. So, I had come home to die. What else was left for me? Alcohol had taken my will, my thinking, and my spirit. All that was left was my body.

The Korean War had taught me about dying. Many of my friends died there. That was also when my drinking started. Drinking was encouraged in the military, and at the time it worked—muting feelings such as fear, shame, and guilt. Drinking also slowed the thoughts of what happened and what might happen, dulled the mind to be able to face another day, month, and year. After the war, it was too late. Addiction had set in along with denial, blame, and transference all covering the core of the problem—my deep anger and inability to forgive and move on.

I had been raised with my grandparents and my parents. At the age of five, I was taken away to a Catholic boarding school where I was to learn not to be Native-American in the harsh, inflexible surroundings. I was not allowed to speak my language, and my lips were snapped with a rubber band if I was caught.

The night I returned home I heard an owl, and as I lay alone I prayed for God to help me. In our tribal tradition when one hears an owl, it could mean death. During the night, I dreamed a very powerful dream. In the dream my ancestors had come back, taken me on horseback, and shown me what I had to do. When I awoke in a cold sweat, I was afraid. I knew I must get the help of a Medicine person. I went to my aunt who knew of these things, and I asked her advice. She helped me.

Next, I went to an *iyeska* (Interpreter-Healer), made an offering, and requested his assistance. At his home, he prepared for a ceremony, obtained food for everyone to eat afterward, and gifts for those performing. Relatives were invited to support me, and they helped as they could, with cooking and prayers. This was done, and the *iyeska* with his assistants, singers, and others all prayed in the old way.

My friends and close relatives came to support me and to pray. The *iyeska* explained to me that in my circle I had created a coyote. I would not look at this coyote, and so this coyote kept biting me, tearing at me. If I wanted to change, I must face the coyote and honor him. In this way, the coyote could no longer sneak up and bite me. "The way you honor what you have created is by owning it," the *iyeska* said. Then the *iyeska* gave me instructions for the coming year—to pray, to prepare a sweat lodge, to make a pipe, and to go away.

I went away, but not willingly. I went to a treatment center called Hazelden. It was at Hazelden that I had another deep spiritual experience. I had been praying in my room, looking out my sliding glass doors at the setting sun with deep red, pink, and purple sky and clouds. In my mind I heard, "When the clouds and the earth come together, when the red disappears with the setting sun, you need never drink again."

I slept, awakening later that night during a powerful spring storm. Looking out into the night, I saw my ancestors in the clouds—standing tall, singing, and drumming for me, happy to have me back in their circle. The next day, a small bird stood outside the sliding glass door. I opened the door, but the bird stayed. I found some breadcrumbs and fed the bird. I knew something had changed, and now began my future without alcohol—a new way of life.

Today I have experienced twenty-three years of sobriety. I practice some of the old ways such as the *inipi* (sweat lodge) and other ceremonies. I go weekly to both AA meetings and to the Catholic Church I was raised in. I have helped myself, my family, and countless others. I'll never forget the words of the healer, "The way you honor what you have created is by owning it." Until I

could own my anger, resentments, and alcoholism—
honor what I had created—I couldn't let go and move
on.

WHEN WE FORGIVE WE BECOME
OUR OWN GOOD PHYSICIAN, AND
THE REMEDY WE USE PERCOLATES
FROM THE WARM, BEATING HEART
OF THE UNIVERSE. WE ARE WORK-
ING WITH THE HEALING ENERGY OF
THE CREATOR. . . . THIS IS WHY
FORGIVENESS DOES A GOOD THING
FOR THE PERSON WHO WRONGED
US ONLY IF IT DOES ITS FIRST GOOD
WORK INSIDE OURSELVES.

Louis Smedes

Forgive When You're Ready, Not When They're Sorry

FORGIVENESS . . . WAS NOT MERE
RELIGIOUS SENTIMENTALITY;
IT WAS AS FUNDAMENTAL A LAW OF
THE HUMAN SPIRIT AS THE LAW
OF GRAVITY.
IF ONE BROKE THE LAW OF GRAVITY
ONE BROKE ONE'S NECK;
IF ONE BROKE THIS LAW OF
FORGIVENESS, ONE INFLICTED A
MORTAL WOUND ON ONE'S
SPIRIT.

Laurens van der Post

Divergent emotions and motivations face us when we choose to forgive someone when they deeply hurt us. But forgiveness has potent power. It is a power to help restore equity and balance within ourselves and, possibly, with those who have harmed us.

When we are gravely hurt, whether through abuse, betrayal, despising, ridicule, insult, prejudice, or a host of other means, it is necessary to take the time we need to evaluate just what happened and then to take action. The two most precious and elusive commodities in our lives are time and peaceful space. We need to take stock of both of them when we're hurting. We need to take sufficient time for close examination in a place of serenity and safety.

Some former school teachers vacation in the same town that I do. It seems that long ago their school superintendents strongly encouraged them to accept early retirement packages. It was, as they say, a deal they couldn't refuse. They are now well into their seventies. Nevertheless, everyone in the little tourist haven knows about how cheated the teachers still feel about the "rule of 59 years," the age they were "forced" to retire. The postman knows about them being "cheated." The rotary club and bridge club hear about it at their monthly meetings. The summer visitors at church hear about it. Everyone murmurs sympathy the first time they hear it, but makes sure they run the other way when they see "old retired-teacher so and so" coming their way. The old retirees live their bitterness, sleep with it, and may just die with it if they don't choose to let go. They're in danger of waiting too long.

At some point we need to close the books on our anger and bitterness. Either that or we condemn ourselves to becoming a prisoner of it. We must choose our own time to do what we have decided.

I'm not just talking about those of us who are highly sensitive. When we've been hurt, all of us react with shock and disbelief. This is a common protective defense our egos provide to shield us from pain. If, for example, we immediately forgive someone who has betrayed us while we are still in a state of shock, our forgiveness will only mask the pain of humiliation that will certainly surface later when triggered by a similar event. It follows then that healing the pain is an elusive and prolonged process. Moreover, the pain goes deeper and is more exacerbated because it is dealt with in a way that is neither respectful of the time we need nor of our personal dignity that was assaulted when the pain was inflicted.

To put it another way, the question is whether forgiveness is appropriate at all. Sometimes we rush into premature offers or acceptance of forgiveness out of obedience to what we understand religion or family values have taught us to do. We rush into acts of forgiveness because we don't want "the sun to go down on our anger." When this is coupled with an impulse to get rid of the pain we feel, the outcome is a disaster to our psychic and spiritual well-being. Many of us take a black and white view of anger and believe that it is always a sin. Therefore, it follows under this logic that it must be evicted from our minds and souls immediately.

Another reason many, if not most of us, too quickly accept offers of forgiveness is to avoid confrontation, and to get things back to the equal footing we were on before. Or, we think that forgiveness will keep the offender at bay—preferably far away from us. Avoiding confrontation in this way severs any intimacy that may have existed between us.

There is a memorable scene in the movie *A River Runs Through It,* based on the boyhood memories of the writer Norman Maclean. In the scene, we see the two brothers return from a harrowing whitewater ride down the rapids of the Chute River. They and their friends put each other up to a life-or-death dare to "shoot the 'Chute'" in a boat "borrowed" from a neighbor. There were only two problems. The boys didn't ask their neighbor's permission to take the boat. Second, they ran the river without their parents' knowledge or permission, knowing that their parents would never allow them to take such a risk. As the scene unfolds, the boys wreck the boat and almost lose their lives in the effort. Their elation over besting the rapids with their lives intact turns to disgrace when they face their father's wrath and punishment the minute they return home.

The two brothers' shame about their father's disappointment in them turns to blaming one another, which then erupts into an all-out punching, gouging, and swearing fistfight. The fight effectively severs their close relationship. Even worse, horrified by the fighting, their mother tries to stop them by interposing her own body between them. In the melee, their mother is punched to the ground. Only then does the fighting stop.

What follows is silence. Then, a denial by their mother that anything has happened. The message is that confrontation is beneath them. It's vulgar, coarse, and cheap. We Macleans don't do this! The shame, self-denigration, and bitterness that follow forbid authentic intimacy. The incident shapes the brothers' relationship from then on. It goes from an open, honest enjoyment of each other to one of false fronts covering wariness.

If "fast forgiveness" can act as a shield that our egos put up to defend against pain, shame and guilt are its close cousins. Whereas guilt relates to an act we did or an omission, shame involves the whole person and relates to a tension between who you are and who you aspire to be. In this tension, if we defend ourselves against shame with rage, powerlessness, or power, then it's an easy stretch to include fast forgiveness as a form of defense against shame. As fast forgivers, we may very well be utilizing forgiveness as a way to exert power over someone or achieve a righteous posture. If that is achieved, we can exert "moral superiority" over the one we forgive.

If we forgive to manipulate and gain a moral advantage over someone, we are being profoundly self-deceptive. Fast forgiveness will only make matters worse. Now, instead of being the oppressed, we become the oppressor, the judge, jury, and executioner. This sort of phony forgiveness robs us from claiming freedom from the one we judge, and we become even more firmly bound to the one who has hurt us.

The power to forgive is in our hands when we are ready, not when the other person says he or she is sorry. To claim the power of forgiveness is ours to choose at the right time for us. The reason the power belongs to us is that we are the ones who are injured. We are the only ones who can accurately describe what has been done to or taken from us. It is in our hands to activate the power that is already in our life. The one who hurt us may say they are sorry, but if we're not ready to name the disappointment, degradation, wound, or shame, and move on, then we are not ready to forgive and let go.

Another reason that the power of forgiveness remains with us, the injured, comes down to two hard facts: First, they may apologize readily simply to get off the hook, salve their conscience, but have little intention of changing their behavior. If we forgive at their pace, nothing is solved for us or them. Second, they may never say they're sorry. So, if we wait for them to come to us before we decide to forgive, we will not be released from the shackles of pain that we so very much deserve to have broken.

The bottom line is that we must forgive when we are ready. We forgive for our health of spirit, body, and mind—not because our forgiveness will change the other person—though that can be hoped for. We forgive to bring what healing we can to a broken world, and we can do so honestly only when we know that the moment has arrived. We need to forgive, but it must be from our heart and in our time.

FORGIVENESS WOULD HAVE TO COME OR WE ALL WILL BE DESTROYED. BUT NOT YET, NOT UNTIL VIOLENCE HAS BECOME JUSTICE, LAWLESSNESS BECOME ORDER, AND WAR HAS BECOME PEACE.

Dietrich Bonhoeffer

Forgive When You're Ready, Not When They're Sorry

- My Native-American grandfather warned that we will become what we are attached to and won't let go of. Here are some questions to ask yourself to determine if you have held on too long to your anger and need to move now to forgiveness:

  - Am I absorbing and reflecting the very things I despise in my enemy?

  - Am I becoming someone worse?

  - Am I losing my real self?

- Examine these warning signs to see if you've become attached to the enemy or the incident. Ponder them and see if they apply:

  - Someone close to you has told you that you are too obsessed with (name of the enemy).

  - You go to bed thinking about your enemy and wake up with them on your mind. You think about them as often as you used to think about people or things in which you take joy.

  - Every movie or book with a villain/hero plot gets recast with your enemy playing the lead role of the villain. You play the victim.

  - Because your friends and family will no longer listen to your complaints about your enemy, you enlist others who will sympathize with you.

  - You cannot release yourself of the pain your enemy has caused without losing your shackled sense of identity.

FORGIVENESS HAS MANY LAYERS,
MANY SEASONS. . . . THE IMPOR-
TANT PART OF FORGIVENESS IS TO
BEGIN AND TO CONTINUE. THE FIN-
ISHING OF IT ALL IS A LIFE WORK.

Clarissa Pinkola Estes

I Would Change Places

Their letters crossed in the mail. In early June 1997, nineteen-year-old Mario Ramos, from his cell in Chicago's Cook County Jail, wrote a letter to Stephen and Maurine Young, the parents of Andrew Young, also nineteen, the youth he had murdered one year before. "If it was possible," he wrote, "I would change places with your son and die in his place instead. But there is no action you or I can take to bring back Andrew or change what has been done. Though I could spend the rest of my life in jail, I don't come close to the hurt your family must be going through. I hope that some way you may find it in your heart to forgive me."

Even as he wrote, Andrew Young's mother, miles away, was typing a letter to Mario: "You don't know me, though I suspect you've heard of me. I am Maurine, Andrew's mom. I've thought about you and prayed for you many times since the day you shot and killed my son." She wrote in some detail of her own struggles in life, then concluded, "You've probably heard Jesus is the way, the truth, and the life. I'm writing to tell you it's true: If he is for you, who can be against you? Well, I don't know if you'd ever be up to asking my forgiveness for killing my son, so I'll go first. I forgive you!"

This apology and forgiveness, spontaneous on both sides, struck a chord in the community of Evanston, Illinois, where both youths had been raised. The local newspaper ran a series of stories and marveled editorially at the extraordinary nature of "the emotional healing" the exchange of letters revealed. How, citizens wondered, had it all happened?

The reconciliation was, in fact, no accident. It occurred in large measure because of the sustained outreach by parishioners of the local Catholic church the Ramos family attended and the members of the Evanston Bible Church where the Young's worshiped.

The murder was committed on June 17, 1996, on the border between Chicago and Evanston, a large, mostly middle-class suburb that has seen an increase in drugs and gang activity during the previous ten years. Mario Ramos, a slightly built, shy, bespectacled youth, was standing with a group of his fellow Latin King gang members near a fruit store on the Chicago side of the border when a car containing two white and two black youths pulled up. The driver, Andrew Young, waited while his twin brother Sam entered the store to cash a check. Mario ran past the waiting car and reportedly flashed a gang sign. When the car's occupants failed to respond appropriately, the Latin Kings felt insulted.

As the auto pulled away, Mario and an older companion gave chase on a bicycle—a chase that would have been futile if the car had not been stopped by a traffic light at a busy intersection two blocks away.

Mario got off his bike, took a pistol supplied by his partner, ran up to the waiting car, and fired a single shot. It struck Andrew in the left arm, tore through his heart, and exited his right side. By the time Andrew's frantic companions drove him to the hospital, he was beyond help. Mario and his associates were chased down by the police and charged with murder.

At St. Nicholas Church, the pastor, Father Robert Oldershaw, preached on Sunday about the incident. "A terrible thing has happened," he said. "Two families have been touched by tragedy. How do we as a parish respond?"

His personal response was to begin visiting Mario, whom he found at first overwhelmed with remorse and self-pity. He only meant to wound the driver, Mario said, in order to prove himself a worthy Latin King. Oldershaw called together leaders of the local Hispanic community, which had come as a group to the church several years before when their old church was closed. A parish Hispanic council was formed, and for the first time, the parish, city officials, and local police collaborated to better serve the special needs of Hispanic citizens.

Week after week Oldershaw updated parishioners about these developments, weaved the latest news into his sermons, urged parishioners to break barriers between Anglos and Hispanics, and asked for prayers for the two families affected by the tragedy. In particular, he urged the people to write or visit Mario in prison, thus initiating an ongoing string of contacts between the churchgoing faithful and the self-confessed killer. Many wrote and several visited; two in fact, went to see Mario almost weekly for an entire year while his case was continued in court. As months passed, the jail chaplain, Ron De Rose, reported a gradual change in the youth. "He was transformed, truly repentant," De Rose says. "We don't see that very often in here. I think Mario's faith is genuine."

Oldershaw contacted the Youngs and asked if they wanted to talk. They were wary at first. Their own pastor, the Reverend Stephen McCorkle, had reached out to them, and the church members had been bringing in food and easing them through the shock. But soon a kind of friendship developed between Andrew's parents and the Catholic pastor.

"We talked and talked," says Stephen Young, a piano technician whose face still reflects his deep anguish. "For a long time, I'll admit I would have killed Mario," he says. "I was entangled in vengeance. I could not feel love in any way." Nevertheless, he attended one of Mario's court hearings and was introduced by Oldershaw to Mario's mother, who spoke little English. The two stricken parents sat beside each other on the courtroom bench for many minutes. They held hands and both wept.

In the months after the murder, Stephen turned his attention toward gun control. He became a leader in efforts to ban handguns or at least change state laws that permit easy gun purchase. He organized marches and letter-writing campaigns to legislators.

Maurine Young, meanwhile, reflected on her own life. A former Catholic, she had been rescued from depression many years before by two evangelical women who helped her, she says, "to recommit my life to Jesus." Now she pondered what more that recommitment required in this awful circumstance. As the date of the sentencing approached, she decided to take action. She wrote the letter to Mario, she says, because she made a promise to the women who helped restore her faith that henceforth God "would be the king of my life, my boss, pilot, leader, high priest. He would run the show." She had scarcely mailed the letter when Mario's letter arrived at her home.

In July 1997, Mario appeared in criminal court for sentencing. Oldershaw was among those who asked the judge for mercy. "I firmly believe that Mario's life need not be lost," he says. "It can be saved, it is being saved. Many people have participated in this saving." But the judge said the nature of the crime left little room for flexibility. He handed down a sentence of forty years, far less than the maximum possible. But because of an Illinois truth-in-sentencing provision, Mario must be incarcerated for the full sentence making him eligible for release in 2036 when he will be fifty-eight years old.

In October, both Stephen Young and Oldershaw appeared at the Evanston march and rally inaugurating a campaign against teen violence. The priest told the crowd of 1,000 that the campaign would succeed only if it included the major ingredient of reconciliation between aggrieved parties, and he related again the now familiar story of the letters that crossed in the mail.

Robert McClory

THERE IS A RIGHT MOMENT TO FORGIVE. . . . HOW FAST IS FAST, HOW SLOW IS SLOW NO ONE CAN TELL US. ONLY YOU THE HURTING PERSON WILL KNOW WHEN THE RIGHT TIME HAS COME.

Louis Smedes

March Is a Time of Remembering

March is the time my brother and I particularly remember Mom and Dad. They both died during this month—Mom, fifteen years ago; Dad, five years ago. My brother and I generally speak on the phone several times during the month. We share stories. Something Mom said. Something Dad did. The memories are more gentle as the time passes. Sometimes we share with chagrin something we wished we hadn't said or done. And sometimes with sadness something Dad said or did.

"Have you ever really forgiven Dad?" I asked my brother during a recent phone call.

"Yeah. Didn't I ever tell you how it happened?" he replied.

He proceeded to tell me how over time he slowly and cautiously let go of his anger toward Dad for the abuse and emotional abandonment he endured over the years.

Our dad suffered from a variety of mental illnesses beginning in his childhood. When my brother was six and I was two, Dad was diagnosed as a schizophrenic and was briefly hospitalized. The next time he finally saw a doctor for his disorders, ending up in a state hospital, it was seventeen years later and the diagnosis had evolved to manic depression. During those intervening years and even the years to follow, Dad could be violent, but mostly he was depressed. What we experienced as his children was primarily a dad who was moody, who couldn't be depended upon, and who was so self-absorbed that he didn't seem to be interested in our lives. There were moments of real "daddy" experiences, but the temper or depressed gaze through a cloud of cigarette smoke seemed to overshadow the good times.

My brother left home when he was nineteen and I was fifteen. I really didn't know how he felt about Dad at that time. All I knew was that he had made it out of the house and seemed to be successful, at least in the eyes of my mother. It wasn't until my mother's death that I learned how deeply Dad had affected my brother; how strong my brother's anger was toward Dad.

My brother's rage at times could be palpable. Over the years after Mom died, my brother felt his only duty toward Dad was to provide for his room and board and medical care at the senior's home and nursing facility. Unfortunately, Dad wanted more than that and would call both of us three or four or five times a day. The conversations would range from a short greeting followed by silence, to a laundry list of complaints that we were supposed to take care of from hundreds of miles away. My brother paid Dad's bills and that contributed to my brother's anger. Dad would order some expensive electronic toy over the phone, the bill appearing on the credit card. However, within my brother's anger was a desire to give Dad some sense of independence as his world became more and more restricted. So the credit card stayed and the frustrations continued.

On the other hand, my response to Dad was not so much anger as hurt. Right after Mom died, I exploded into a rage at Dad for taking all important people and things from me. However, I was mainly hurt and even felt responsible for the way Dad was. I often thought that I should have been able to do something to make him better. In truth, there probably was an undercurrent of anger toward Dad for robbing me of my childhood. I always seemed to be taking care of him. Never the other way around.

Dad died ten years after Mother, and it took most of those ten years for me to come to a place of forgiveness. Actually it probably was about five or six years after Mom's death that I finally began a process that allowed me to let go of my anger. That's not to say I wasn't frustrated over Dad's behavior and at times angry when he would be so demanding. However, I slowly began to accept Dad for who he could be, not for who I hoped he would be.

We never had a great confrontation. I never even talked with Dad about the painful memories and their effect on my life. I just slowly stopped trying to change him. I began to have regular conversations with him, telling him of my daily activities. When he would slip into some mild psychotic behavior, I would let him talk it out instead of trying to talk him out of wherever he found himself at the time. I would try to make him feel safe, without analyzing or fixing.

My final moment of forgiveness and reconciliation came the December before his death. It was really a major moment of grace. I went out to visit Dad in early December. On the plane, I told myself over and over to have no expectations, no plans for fixing things. I reflected on Dad's life with Mom and thought about what he always wanted Mom to do for him. And then it came to me. Dad simply wanted her to sit with him. She would grade papers in the same room or work on a project with Dad sitting nearby. They probably didn't talk much. Dad just felt safe with Mom nearby. So I decided I would just be present for Dad.

And so I was. We would sit in his room or go out on the balcony where he could smoke a cigarette. We would sit in silence, comfortable with each other's presence. Dad would make a comment about something one of the residents did or ask me what I was working on at home. We would talk about past events, gentle times, not the bad times. We laughed. After all the years of pain and struggle, we had our father-daughter moment.

My brother's journey seemed to be similar. About four years after Mother died, during one of the many phone calls to my brother, Dad asked him how he was doing. Dad wanted to know what he was working on. My brother's usual thoughts when Dad tried to be father was "I'll make sure you're cared for but don't think you can start being a father to me now." However, his sharp retort died on his tongue. He responded by slowly telling Dad what he was doing. The papers he was working on, what projects he was involved in. Over the remaining years of Dad's life, he became father to my brother in the best way he knew how. Stumbling. Not always successful. But it seems that my brother and my dad also began having reasonable conversations scattered among the paranoia and depression.

My brother also had his moment before Dad died. The Friday before his death, Dad had called my brother and complained about a cold that seemed to be making him really feel bad. My brother started to ask questions about it, but Dad then played it down and asked if my brother had finished a paper he was working on. The rest of the conversation was about what my brother was doing. And it seemed my father listened.

For both of us, forgiveness wasn't one moment of confrontation. Even though we may have had more good times if it had come earlier, I don't think it could have happened in any other time frame. Although we knew we had been injured by my father, both my brother and I had to discover what the damage really was before we could move on. We had to grow up so we could experience Dad as the father he could be amidst his self-absorption and mental disorders. We were gifted with grace moments that have allowed us, along with the pain and sadness, to remember our father with love and gentleness years after his death.

Rosalie Hooper-Thomas

FORGIVENESS IS PRIMARILY FOR OUR OWN SAKE, SO THAT WE NO LONGER CARRY THE BURDEN OF RESENTMENT.

Thich Nhat Hanh

WAY 9 :

Make an Act of Forgiveness

FORGIVENESS . . . DOES NOT MEAN
GIVING UP ONE'S PROTECTION, BUT
ONE'S COLDNESS. . . .YOU ARE FREE
TO GO.

IT MAY NOT HAVE TURNED OUT
TO BE A *HAPPILY EVER AFTER*, BUT MOST
CERTAINLY THERE IS NOW A FRESH
ONCE UPON A TIME WAITING FOR YOU
FROM THIS DAY FORWARD.

Clarissa Pinkola Estes

L et's suppose the time has come when we are ready
to forgive someone who has made us angry. We've
taken all the time we need. We've been respectful of our
own integrity. We've also named the violation, perhaps
with the help of strong companions, spiritual guides,
trusted friends, counselors, or attorneys. We've
explored the options available to us and the lessons
learned in the process. At this point, we may feel that we
need to meet with the one who inflicted the wound of
betrayal, abandonment, or shame—and forgive them.

125

Some counselors would urge that meeting with our enemy is a required step in "getting closure" or claiming the full liberation available through forgiveness. They argue that freedom from resentment can be had if, but only if, we sit down with the one who inflicted the suffering and tell the person how we have been betrayed, shamed, physically hurt, and so on. Once we are sure that the other person comprehends our pain, only then in this view can we forgive. These counselors would claim that we are cheating ourselves and the process of forgiveness if we don't do this.

I believe that many counselors, with all good intentions, are confusing forgiveness with reconciliation. For most of us, forgiveness is possible and necessary, and something we can accomplish on our own. Reconciliation may be desirable, but takes both parties to accomplish. In short, if we demand reconciliation, we may never reach closure and peace because our offender may indefinitely rebuff us. Then we doom ourselves to walk a fog-shrouded path in limbo. After all, if we could only reach a place of peace and joy again by reconciling, we could never reach this state with deceased offenders. I disagree with the school of thought that requires us to sit down with the offender.

Facing our offender and trying to reach reconciliation with forgiveness is admirable, but optional. Reconciliation implies a return to mutual agreement and harmonious co-existence, to bring both persons back to the place where they once were. To paraphrase Archbishop Desmond Tutu, "Forgiveness needs one; reconciliation takes two." Forgiveness is a necessary step on the journey to reconciliation, but is also a fine destination in itself.

Forgiveness basically means to set aside our anger with another. This is not a "cop-out." It is not half-baked reconciliation or an abortion of the process. Forgiveness, the Dalai Lama tells us, is also the companion to compassion. In being compassionate and living in loving kindness with each other, we are radiating the love of God.

The Latin root of the word "compassion" means "to suffer with." The Sanskrit root of "compassion" likewise means "to suffer with," but takes the meaning one step further. It also means "to suffer with and to suspend all joy." Furthermore, to take the step on the road to compassion, the Dalai Lama points out, we are invited to forgive. "Forgiveness," he observed, "means to suspend ill will against the one that hurt or harmed you."

Many times, forgiveness is possible, but reconciliation is not. Moreover, there are other times when we can forgive the person, but it is not possible to tell them about it. We may need to keep it to ourselves for several reasons.

A meeting might simply dig up the old dirt and start the trouble again, only making matters far worse. One example comes immediately to mind. A friend of mine had been virtually left out of her father's will because, the father said, "you're single and don't have any kids. Your brother needs the money more than you do." Anger and hurt burned inside her for years. Finally she sought some counseling and, having come to some resolution inside, was advised to face her mother who had agreed with the father's decision. My friend felt ready to end the bitterness and estrangement with her mother. She recounted the ensuing disaster.

After describing her bitterness about the father's will and the mother's agreement, using "I" messages, not blaming her mother but expressing her feelings, she finally said, "Mom, I forgive you for not supporting me in this."

Her mother stared at her in shock, "What do you mean, 'forgive me'? You should be asking for pardon after giving me the cold shoulder all these years. Do you realize how embarrassed I was when you didn't come to your brother's anniversary party?"

"Mom, you're the one who almost never called. And, my loving brother never sent me an invitation. You invited me at the end of a phone call just a couple of days beforehand."

"Money, money. That's all you wanted from your father."

The conversation suddenly turned into a replay of the bitter recriminations that had robbed my friend of peace for all those years. In seeking reconciliation, wounds were reopened and new wounds inflicted.

Unfortunately, many of us have lived through a variation of this scene. The point is that despite good intentions we may be unable to effectively communicate our heart-filled wish to forgive. The other person may be unable to hear what we're saying and surprised, even shocked, that we were carrying a bag full of resentments. He or she may wonder what other resentment and pain we're carrying. They may be on their guard with us in the future. Best to let it go.

There are other times when keeping forgiveness to yourself is the choice of discretion over what you think is valor. The person who hurt you may be seriously ill or simply elderly. Now may not be the time or place to resurrect events or actions that give rise to the offer and acceptance of forgiveness. The person who hurt you may be dead, in parts unknown, or simply unreachable. It puts them out of range for an active exchange of forgiveness.

The person who hurt you may not be capable of receiving your offer of forgiveness and may use the occasion as an opportunity to inflict additional harm on you or others. In this instance, you would be jeopardizing yourself unnecessarily.

So, if you have:

- come to grips with your anger,
- sorted out the responsibility for the offense,
- given up your right to revenge,
- decided that you want to forgive,
- tried to see your enemy as a fellow human,
- and taken the time you need,

then you are probably ready to forgive.

If you *do* feel safe and are reasonably sure that either approach might be effective, you may choose to meet the person face-to-face or send a letter offering forgiveness. Sometimes the offender will offer you a sign that they wish to be forgiven. You receive an invitation to a gathering. They include you in some project that they know you're interested in. They apologize in some way. In these instances, you still need to weigh your options, but offering forgiveness directly might be helpful.

If you do meet, first become reacquainted. Ask about the person, their family, their accomplishments. Express any genuine appreciation you might have for the other person. Bring humor to play if that seems natural for the two of you. Offer a few words of forgiveness, but don't belabor the point by repeating it over and over. If the other person talks about it, fine, but you've said what you need to. Move on.

If you cannot meet for a variety of reasons or choose not to, write a letter to the person, offering forgiveness. You don't need to send it. Or, ask a trusted, sensitive friend to sit in the place of the one you wish to forgive. Request that they just listen and be there with you as you say the healing words. And, in instances like this, performing some closure ritual can be especially helpful (the next chapter offers some advice about forgiveness rituals).

Having reached this point, act. Make a decision for life: make an act of forgiveness to help you displace or remove your anger.

FORGETTING IS SOMETHING THAT TIME TAKES CARE OF, BUT FORGIVENESS IS AN ACT OF VOLITION, AND ONLY THE SUFFERER IS QUALIFIED TO MAKE THE DECISION.

William Carlos Williams

Make an Act of Forgiveness

- Bring to mind three examples of persons whom you trusted who later hurt you. What has each taught you about forgiveness in your life? Next, think about a similar dilemma with a friend, family member, or colleague. What does that person—in this painful situation—teach you about forgiveness?

- Choose a space in a comfortable chair where you can be alone and undisturbed for at least fifteen minutes. Relax, close your eyes, take three deep breaths, and then breathe normally.

  Imagine you are walking through a sunlit glade in the woods. As you ascend the path, you come to a ledge where you are able to sit on a sandstone bench and take your rest. As you look to your right, you see a bronze plaque. As you read the plaque closely it says: "This is dedicated to (*your name*) and the lesson you learned in (for example, compassion, patience, simplicity) from (*name the person who hurt you*). Continue your journey upward, reading plaques along the way, until you reach the last lesson.

  See yourself as you are now. Ask your defending angel to help you see yourself as precious in the sight of the Creator. Thank the Holy One for this vision of yourself.

  When you are ready, descend down the path and return to the beginning of the path. Let yourself be fully relaxed, free, and serene. As you wish, slowly stretch your arms and legs, take three deep breaths, and open your eyes.

- If you are willing, close your eyes and take three deep, relaxing breaths. Release all thoughts of resentment and betrayal to the person who hurt you. Imagine that the Creator, the one who forgives and heals, bathes you in the sweet, warm ointment of joy.

  Thank your Creator-God by spontaneously expressing your gratitude for coming to a place of forgiveness and power. You may repeat these words for meditation: "You have poured your strength into me so that I may be healed and live to be a co-creator with you to transform the world into a loving community. Fill my heart with kind forgiveness."

*   Make some act of forgiveness. Consider these two options:

    *   If meeting with the person is possible, safe, and desirable, do so.

    *   If you choose not to meet, perhaps write and send a letter or note that expresses your forgiveness. It need not be long. Be at peace with the fact that you may not receive a reply.

If you do not choose the first two options, write an unsent letter of forgiveness or offer forgiveness with a friend, substituting for the person you wish to forgive.

Whichever way you make your act of forgiveness, put closure on the journey to forgiveness by performing some ritual. See Way 10 for help.

FORGIVENESS IS LOVE PRACTICED AMONG PEOPLE WHO LOVE POORLY. IT SETS US FREE WITHOUT WANTING ANYTHING IN RETURN.

Henri J. M. Nouwen

Jack

"Who is that man at the back of the parking lot?" my best friend, Nan, asked. "He's dressed in a black suit and tie and he's so pale, he looks like a ghost!" I followed her gaze and saw my father's friend, Jack, standing far away from the throng of mourners exiting the church vestibule after my father's funeral.

The large assembly of mourners huddled together, holding hands, or hugging each other. My father and Jack were in fact close friends. But they were also business competitors. Both men were of a generation of smart, technically gifted engineers who could, after the end of World War II, get into the road and bridge construction business with a little investment capital. Those who were as bold and fearless as they were talented, prospered. Some more than others.

On more than a few "jobs" that were available, my father and another contractor would join their efforts. Subcontracts would be awarded so that one would do the road building and the other would build bridges. When Jack, among others, was either the subcontractor or the main contractor, the public got a result that was as economical as it was sound.

Despite their competitiveness, there was a true affection and admiration for the other. They became social friends; hunting, fishing, and golfing together. As I grew to be a competitive golfer, I often was invited to join them on the course so I got to witness their boisterous friendship up close. For example, as my father prepared to drive his golf ball off the first tee, Jack would yell, "Hit the hell out of it, Charlie!" My father's jaw would clench and his arms and shoulders would tense as he prepared to slug the ball as hard and as far as he could. Of course, in his determination to hit it 350 yards, my father would tense up and "top" the ball so it would bloop and bounce off the tee.

Not to be outdone, my dad would wait until Jack hovered over his putt on the ninth green to say, "If you make this, Jack, you'll be one up on me!" With that, Jack would over-stroke the putt and helplessly watch as the ball rolled to the other end of the green, taking another two putts to get it in the hole. My dad would then calmly stroke his putt into the middle of the cup and usually be the victor in our matches.

Then came the day when my father could no longer keep pace with Jack in the business world. Jack pursued national and international business. On his sorties home, he invited our family over to his new multi-million dollar house. He flew my father and some other friends to remote fishing or hunting spots in his own plane. He began to appear with celebrities at matches. My father, on the other hand, took a different path. He became involved in public service at the same time as he reorganized his company. In the early 1960s my father was elected national director of the contractor's association and became a national arbitrator in labor disputes.

He and Jack saw less and less of each other. One day, Jack called out of the blue. "Charlie, I need to see you right away." My dad said he'd be glad to meet Jack for lunch, but Jack said he didn't really have time. They got together for coffee instead.

My dad said the intensity and desperation in Jack's eyes startled him. Always a casual smoker, Jack lit one Camel cigarette after another as he got directly to the point. "I need a loan."

Although my father was surprised at this request, he never hesitated. "How much do you need, Jack?"

"I guess about $200,000 would get me back on track," said Jack.

Since my father was taking home about $35,000 a year, and the rest of his capital was tied up in equipment and salaries, Jack's figure had the effect of a rabbit punch. "I can write a check for $2,000 right now if that will help, Jack. But I don't have that kind of capital. What I can do is make some calls to some bankers I know or some investors."

Jack said he'd already gone that route. He was deeply in debt and about to lose everything. The story Jack told was a tragic one. In a few years, he had had his savings siphoned off in bad investments and marginal inventions that new friends and long-lost relatives and in-laws brought to him. If that weren't enough, Jack's marriage of twenty-six years was over.

This was the day of my parents' thirty-fifth wedding anniversary, and Jack knew it. My dad listened to his story and, in the end, co-signed some notes to help Jack get on his feet again. The fact is, my father was having a difficult business year himself.

During the months that followed, my father was pained by the tension Jack showed any time they were in the same room together. Invitations to play golf or go fishing were refused, "I'm just too busy" was the usual excuse. Then came a series of snubs that caused a rift in their friendship. I was there when it happened. Jack would call and invite us to play golf and have dinner. He'd set the time. We'd get to the first tee, and Jack would be nowhere to be seen. No message left, or pale excuses like, "Oh, something came up," or "I forgot."

The third time this happened, the starter at the first golf tee said, "Oh, Mr. Jack finished the round with the others a long time ago. They're probably back at the grill. That's where they usually go." My father asked me to wait while he talked to Jack.

He came out to the car as angry as he was sad. "The lesson in this," he told me, "is that when you give money to someone, don't have an agenda. Don't expect that they'll pay you back either in money or in kind. That's what I think the Bible means when it says to lend so that your left hand doesn't know what the right hand is doing. Sometimes—and this is the hardest part—the person you reach out to will resent the fact that you could help them, but resent even more that they had to *ask* you for help. It makes them feel as if your friendship is no longer an equal one. They'll push you away."

"So Jack resents the help you gave him?" I asked.

"It seems that way," he said sadly.

Ten years later, my father got a call from Jack. They hadn't seen each other since that incident. Jack was in the hospital and said he needed to see my father. My father left for Jack's hospital room as soon as he put down the phone. As he told me later, he was totally unprepared for what he found. Jack, who always had immense energy and the physique of a middleweight boxer, lay in his hospital bed. His bones protruded under his pale, unhealthy looking skin. He was almost bald. The only things unchanged were his penetrating deep blue eyes. As my father entered the spare, sterile hospital room, Jack greeted him by throwing off the blankets and sheets of his bed and drawing his pajama pant leg up from his left ankle. My father was usually unflappable in the face a medical problem of any sort. This was different.

"I had" he said, "all I could do to keep from vomiting." As Jack had thrown the blanket off and lifted his pajama leg, "The smell of rotting flesh filled the room. Jack's foot and leg were a mass of rotten, gray flesh." As he swallowed the bile shooting up from his stomach, my father saw that part of the leg was an open wound. "I could see his tibia," my father recounted.

Determined not to react in a way that would appear to rebuff Jack, my father knelt down next to the rotting limb. "This is the worst thing I've ever seen, Jack! You've got to be in incredible pain."

"I am," Jack said simply.

"Do you want to tell me about this?" Jack did.

That night he told my father about the cancer, the diagnosis, prognosis, and treatment that lay ahead. In the end, Jack said that there was no exit. "This is the final act."

My father asked if there was anything Jack would like him to do. "Just visit, when you can."

"Anything else?" my father asked.

"No," said Jack. "That would be enough."

My father did visit almost every day. Through the chemotherapy, radiation treatments, and rehabilitation days.

To my knowledge, Jack never said, "I'm sorry." For his part, my father never said, "I forgive you." But I am confident both were well aware of how the other felt. They were, again, just happy in each other's company.

That spring, my father faced his own final act. He agreed to a heart bypass procedure that was just being pioneered. He was probably the most vital man many of us have ever known. Consequently, we all were of a frame of mind to expect him to practically dance out of surgery. True to form, he elected it because he felt it would ensure that he could have a longer, healthier life. It was not, as they say, a successful outcome.

As the mourners gathered at the church for his funeral, all expressed disbelief that he was actually gone. Jack couldn't believe that Charlie had gone before him. So when the pastor urged us to tell Charlie's story to each other to help each other mourn and to keep the light of his life alive, we took it to heart. Jack took it to heart.

Jack died eleven months after my father's death. His funeral was on an early spring day. When I came back to my apartment from Jack's simple, loving service, I opened my kitchen window. A robin flew to my windowsill and alighted there. It cocked its head and seemed to give me a penetrating gaze. I felt as though the robin was carrying Jack's spirit.

Then the robin cocked its head at me again, paused, and flew westward toward the bright blue sky.

TWO WORKS OF MERCY SET A MAN
FREE: FORGIVE AND YOU WILL BE
FORGIVEN; AND GIVE AND YOU WILL
RECEIVE.

Augustine of Hippo

Dealing With Mom

My phone rang late one evening as I was preparing for bed. The voice on the other end belonged to my friend Amy. It was at least eleven o'clock on the east coast, and I knew from the lateness of the hour as well as the agitated tone of her voice that she was, as they say, "up against it."

I guessed that she was either calling about a rift with her mother, a frail widow with whom Amy was living, or the heavy demands of her administrative job. It was the former.

It wouldn't be the first time she called me in a despairing state about her mother's demands interfering with Amy's career responsibilities. To complicate matters, Amy's mother had chronic heart problems and had recently suffered a stroke. Amy gave up an international business career and took a loss of income to come home and take care of her mother. Since she was her mother's only living relative she felt an obligation to care for her. "After all," she said once, "Mom sacrificed for the family; now it's my turn to sacrifice for her. I don't want to live a life of regret for what I didn't do for her when she needed me."

Amy didn't have to wait long between career positions. Her international business and government contacts, her skill at securing major grants, and her teaching talent led to several job offers from major research universities. Amy accepted an offer near her mother's home and soon her teaching career was in as rapid an ascent as her business career had been. Initially, Amy was elated. She felt confident about the contributions she could make to the university as well as the international community. Best of all, she thought, she could support her mother who, up to now, had been living on a small pension and social security.

Her elation didn't last long. As much as she tried to stay above politics at the university and concentrate on teaching and writing, the academic politics made for distraction if not insecurity. Amy responded to this pressure by working longer, harder, and smarter.

Amy's mother was not impressed. Whenever Amy accepted invitations to address international conferences or foundation appointments, her mother accused Amy of being heartless and selfish. Amy felt caught between domestic friction and her need to work at a professional level that honored her dedication and ability. So, late at night, Amy called me to vent her frustrations and for insight and support.

Our friendship sprang from our earlier association at a Midwestern college. I had had a hand in recruiting her from industry for an adjunct teaching position there. I was impressed by Amy's ability to bridge scholarship and commerce. The fact that she was a young, strong, African-American leader was an asset both for our faculty and our diverse student community. Amy phoned me because of this relationship and because she knew I faced a similar situation living with my widowed mother. Amy's mother and mine were of the same generation and had both faced cruel discrimination. And, our mothers had learned their tactics in handling us from advanced study in "daughter management" taught by their own mothers!

"I'm at my wits' end!" Amy groaned. "My mother is tottering around asking me to check on her 'meds' again. Just a minute ago she dropped her midnight snack on the floor. I got scared thinking she had another small stroke. But she seems all right. I just lost it! I said, 'Mom, you've got to stay with your routine. I have to pack for my trip to China now and I don't have time for this distraction!' She started to cry and say she was useless and maybe she should just go into a nursing home and not bother me anymore. I felt like such a jerk. I said, 'You're not going into a nursing home, but I need your cooperation.' She does this whenever I leave to go to a meeting or a conference. It's a pattern. You've been through this. What have you done? I mean it; don't soften it for me."

I asked Amy a question: "When you were eight or nine, did you resist when your mom wanted you to do something and you wanted to do something else?"

"Sure," she said. "What does that have to do with it?"

"Getting back," I said. "If you think about it, we were once in a dependent position with our mothers, now it's reversed. It's also about control. And she's lonely. So are you, I suspect, because neither of you has a one and only with whom to share your joys and burdens."

Amy was quiet for a while. "Well, okay, but what have you done in this situation?"

"I remember it well. So here goes. I told my mother, 'I love you too much to live at swords' points with you. I'm sorry I've said things that hurt you or done things that caused you sadness.' Then when I got back from a conference, I promised her we'd find a way to live so that we could just accept each other as we are, not for what we wish the other would be. As it turns out, my mother didn't live much longer. We had time to talk. She was able to share what she valued in me, which was worth more than diamonds. We could also express our love for each other. Amy, I can tell you now that without this candor, we couldn't have shared those precious days." Amy and I ended our conversation as we always do, with a prayer for each other.

I got a call from Amy about a week later. Her voice had its old lilt and sunniness back. "You won't believe what happened after our last conversation and prayer. Two friends from church, one a nurse and one a social worker, came over to give my mother and me a plan to think about. There's an opening at an assisted care facility that caters to people like my mom who need care during the day. It provides exercise, physical therapy, and excursions to museums and plays that my mother has always been interested in. They also found a part-time nurse who can visit Mom when I'm away. They presented it in a way so that my mom had a chance to explore at her leisure. She checked the facilities out and loves it! There's one more thing. I don't really say, 'I'm sorry,' nor does she. But we know. We know. And there's no lack of equal opportunity to say, 'I love you!'"

TO MOVE FROM [NON-FORGIVENESS] TO THE FORGIVENESS DIMENSION WAS LIKE MOVING FROM DARKNESS TO LIGHT. THE FORGIVENESS DIMENSION AFFIRMED THAT IN HOPE AND THE POWER OF GOD OUR LIVES ARE NEVER BEYOND REPAIR.

Doris Donnelly

W A Y   1 0 :

Give Closure to Forgiveness Through Ritual

THE PROGRESS FROM A STANCE OF
ANGER TO A POSITION OF FORGIVE-
NESS IS A POWERFUL MOVEMENT. IT
IS A DANCE THAT LENDS ITSELF TO
RITUAL THAT IS LIFE-GIVING AND
LIFE-ENHANCING.

Ariel Dorfman

Arnold Van Gennep, an anthropologist who wrote about rituals, tells us that he's found that the "life of any individual in any society is a series of passages from one age to another and from one occupation to another." He goes on to say that our passages are marked by ceremonies—rituals whose primary purpose is to support the individual passing from one "defined position to another which is equally well defined."

These rituals of transition, like all rituals, are actions that symbolize a reality beyond the literal meaning of the action. For example, when new presidents take the

145

oath of office, they are doing much more than just saying the words, they are assuming the invisible but real
authority and responsibility that go with the office. The
ritual of oath-taking is the symbolic action signifying
this larger reality.

When seen in this light, a ritual is an invitation to
create our own unique expression in the form of art,
dance, or storytelling in a way that has the effect of
moving us, when we feel marginalized or separated
from our authentic selves, to a reconnection of ourselves back to our home, back to our origins. We are
drawn to ritual because of longing. We are not now
connected to the place where we once called home, nor
are we at home in our bodies. We are not yet in the
place where we want to be. Ritual is a way to bridge or
span that gap.

The ritual passage always requires memory, as
dreadful as the experience of conjuring up past pain
usually is for us. Ritual, if we surrender to it, also
requires the sacrifice of release, of letting go of all that
would keep us fettered to an event or a person that has
kept us from well-being.

Finally, ritual leads us to embrace a new way of living that transforms the past. Without the spirit of surrender, without the ethos that sustains it, ritual is just
ritualism, empty and meaningless. When ritual supports our movement over a bridge, we can put a period
at the end of our story of anger and forgiveness, much
like my Native-American friend who told me how ritual helped build a bridge over his resentment, hurt, and
anger:

The conflict between religions I experienced had a tremendous impact on my emotions and the way I thought. When I attended the Mission, the way of teaching was that the Catholic Church was the only true religion and the Indian Way was "devil worship." At the Mission, they cut the boys' hair and taught the idea that a good Christian was someone who had short hair, good behavior, and always did what he or she was told.

Throughout my growing up, I was taught two ways. I was told by my instructors at the Mission that Christ was present in the tabernacle. But when I was home with my relatives, I was taught that God was in everything and revealed his divinity through his creation, through the animals, and all things—mother earth, plants, and so forth. I was confused and began to know I didn't understand what was going on regarding the God they talked about, so different from the God my grandparents talked about.

My grandfather was the one who told me that "there is only One God, and these Blackrobes (Catholic Jesuits) will one day come to an understanding that we worship the same God. And even though our ways are being pushed aside and rejected, have patience. One day you will see the Indian Ways being embraced by these people of the Church."

And my grandfather's predictions came true. Sure enough, at a much later date, some of the Catholic priests began to participate in the sweat lodge ceremonies. I now see drums taken into the Church. I see the sayings of Black Elk, the cedar and sage introduced into the Church, and my people's songs as well. I see priests learning the native language and saying the Mass in my tongue.

This is a tremendous turn-around. Every time I experience this, I can still hear my grandfather tell me, "It takes time, and if you have patience, they will understand. There's wisdom to the way the old people teach tolerance, patience, and being forgiving. Whatever they do to you, forgive them. Under the principle of the Pipe, it teaches compassion." The Pipe teaches inclusiveness rather than exclusiveness. You can't carry unforgiveness or resentment or hate. We must forgive them.

I know it's easy to say, but, he said, "If you want to live the people's Way, the principle of the Pipe is to be forgiving, to walk the sacred path, to use the Pipe like a cane because we can walk in doubt in between. The Pipe can be used symbolically as a cane because we, all of us, struggle back and forth. If we have it, we will be okay, and we will walk with the Pipe in these ways and be in harmony."

And grandfather continued to go to the Catholic church every Sunday, and in the evening he would smoke the Pipe and sing sacred songs.

Human beings have always, all over the world, used rituals to move from one state of being to another. In journeying from hatred, anger, bitterness, and hurt to forgiveness and peace, ritual provides a bridge.

Your forgiveness ritual need not be complicated, but it should be personal. The symbols and actions you use should speak to your heart, mind, and will. Whatever you do can carry you to a new place, a more life-giving and peaceful place within yourself and with your world.

WE NEED RITUALS THAT ACKNOWL-
EDGE THE IMPORTANCE OF THE
QUEST AND THE CENTRALITY OF
THE SPIRIT, WHICH MAKE THE OUT-
SIDE LIKE THE INSIDE AND THE
ABOVE LIKE THE BELOW.

Christina Baldwin

Give Closure to Forgiveness Through Ritual

- Recall meaningful rituals that served as rites of passage or moments of important transitions for you. Remember the symbols and actions that were part of the ceremony. Also try to recapture in your memory all the feelings associated with the ritual.

- Compose a ritual that will help in your process of letting go of anger and also of forgiveness. Here are some ideas, but adapt them to your unique situation and circumstances.

  - Write the thing the person did to you on strips of paper; make a fire (in a safe fire pit, keep a pail of water nearby) and burn them. As you burn them, bless the person by saying, "I release you; I release me."

  - Find some stones. With a marker, write the offense or hurt on the stones, and then throw the stones into a river or a lake. As you throw them, say, sing, or shout a phrase like: "I set you free, I set me free; I wish you prosperity, I wish me prosperity."

- Take a long ritual bath, sauna, or steam. As you sit in the bath, offer a prayer or sing or chant some favorite song, verse, or hymn that affirms your life and love.

- Plant a tree or perennial flowers. As you do, offer words of forgiveness and pray for your enemy. Nurture the plantings, and as you do pray for continued healing and new life.

- Do some regular act of service to poor people, orphans, homeless people, or victims of crime or oppression. Commit yourself to positive acts of good.

- Visualize a bridge. You are standing on one side where your anguish resides. Imagine that on the other side there lies a beautiful, peaceful new land. What does that land hold for you? Will you take anything or anyone with you? If so, describe it or them. Describe how you would like your life to be in that beautiful place. Feel yourself walking over that bridge and leaving the old ways behind. When you get to the other side, stop, breathe deeply, and let yourself feel whatever feelings come. Then offer these words in harmony with your breathing, "I am loving. I am loved. I am free."

- Act on your ritual. At its conclusion, make one or two small resolutions to do each time the old anger and bitterness threaten to disturb your peace.

> THE HIGHEST SACRIFICE IS A BRO-
> KEN AND CONTRITE HEART . . . AND
> THE MOST BEAUTIFUL THING THAT A
> MAN CAN DO IS TO FORGIVE A
> WRONG.
>
> *Eleazor of Worms*

Going to the Mountaintop

For almost a year, my anger had festered. I had chewed over the day of my firing many times, looking at it from all angles. Always my angle. My boss and the CEO always came out as jerks. I had a laundry list of grievances that seemed to grow as I revived long forgotten slights, their stupid mistakes, and bizarre decisions. Even though I had found my new work in many ways more satisfying, my anger haunted my nights and idle moments.

One day, my wife, who had been patient, endlessly supportive, and completely understanding, finally asked, "When are we going to start charging Greg rent?"

Startled, I realized that I had been growling and complaining again—inside—while not listening to what she had been saying. "It's been that bad, eh?" I asked.

"Honey, maybe it's time to let go of all that. You've been talking about making a retreat out in New Mexico, why not just do it? Could help a lot. You can get Joe and Patrice's place, and we have plenty of frequent-flier miles."

Of course, she was right. I was tired of these unwanted guests in our house too. Anger and bitterness are hostile housemates who take up enormous amounts of space, leave their debris everywhere, stink to high heavens, and never *do* pay rent. So I went to the desert to see what God and I could do about my anger and hurt.

Joe and Patrice's place hugged the Sangre de Cristo Mountains. I had spent time there before, and they were gracious enough to let me come on short notice. I brought some recommended books on forgiveness, my Bible, my journal, and most of all a tremendous yearning to get past this anger. The first several days in the desert were painful to say the least. The only reason I could sleep at night was because I had taken long hikes into the mountains. Between this extra exercise and the altitude, my nights were haunted by furious dreams and wide-awake torments. I rehashed everything: why I was bitter, why they were such bastards, what had gone wrong, how hurt I was, how guilty and shamed I felt, and so on. I also finally owned up to my part in the destruction of what had been a pretty decent working relationship for the first ten years. Reading and rereading scripture passages drew me more and more to tears of regret, a desire for forgiveness, and a heart to forgive.

By Saturday afternoon I felt washed out: that combination of exhaustion, release, surrender, and acceptance. I came back from three hours hiking among the mesas, ate a sandwich for lunch, and then lay down for a quick nap. My friends' black Lab woke me with his barking. I turned over to look at the clock: 4:00 p.m.

I had slept three hours. Too tired to get out of bed, I listened as ground squirrels and jays fussed over the apricots scattered on the ground under a tree so full of fruit that its branches arched, touching the ground.

It struck me that I felt like the tree. My burden had borne me down to the ground too. Harvest time had come. I would either shake off the fruit of this last year of anguish and make something good of it, or it would crack me, the fruit falling to rot. In what must have been one of those mysteriously graced moments, I knew what I must do.

The day before, while rummaging around looking for writing paper, I had uncovered a box of crayons and some newsprint. Now I got up, dressed, and went into the living room. I tore the newsprint into foot-long strips about an inch wide. On each strip I crayoned on the name of either Greg or Patrick or both and then wrote one piece of my anger, bitterness, betrayal, and hurt. At the end of each strip I concluded: For this I forgive you. Pretty soon I had a stack of strips.

When I finished writing out my forgiveness for them, I wrote this message for myself: "For all the stupid, angry memos and e-mails that you hurled at Greg and Patrick, I forgive you." On and on I wrote, working my way through red, green, black, and blue crayons. With a pile of new strips strewn on the desk, I was done.

Early Sunday morning, I strapped on my water bottles and fanny pack filled with my forgiveness strips. Settling my floppy, sweat-stained, cotton hat on my head, I began climbing to my favorite mesa top. Even as I hit the steepest part of the climb I seemed to breathe easier. An old hymn played in my head, and when I hit easier inclines, I first hummed and then sang, "How Can I Keep From Singing":

My life flows on in endless song
Above earth's lamentations
I hear the real though far-off hymn
That hails a new creation.

No storm can shake my inmost calm
While to that Rock I'm clinging
Since Love is Lord of heaven and earth,
How can I keep from singing?

The sun was high in the east when I arrived at the top. I knew what I had to do. I stripped off all my excess clothing except for my hat and boots. I'm still not sure why, but it just felt right to stand mostly bare before God and creation. That's what I wanted to be: stripped of my defenses, my denial, and my anger.

Picking a gnarled, dead piñon tree, I took out my strips of anger and forgiveness. Then I started tying them—one by one—on the dead branches. As I tied each one on, I read it, and declared before God and to myself that I forgave. Before long, tears coursed down my face. I kept on. One by one, reciting the hurt. One by one, surrendering and letting go. It took a long time. When I tied the last strip onto the tree, I stood back, staring silently at all the pieces of my anguish being lifted and tossed in the dry mountain breeze. As I circled the tree, I prayed that as each strip disintegrated under wind, rain, and even snow that my anger, bitterness, guilt, and shame would likewise surrender into compassion and complete release.

Then sheer silence embraced me. It was finished.

The next day I dedicated to thanksgiving, blessings, and gratitude. And, I made some simple resolutions just to remind myself of the wonderful lightness that I felt now. One of them surprised me even as I wrote it down. Every time I thought of Greg or Patrick, I would ask God to bless them. Oh, I would not forget their wrongs, but why not bless them. I had blessings in abundance.

I flew out of Albuquerque on Independence Day, July 4, and the wonder of it was not lost on me. For the first time in months—maybe even years—I felt free of my fear, shame, anger, and bitterness. At least for now, "no storm could shake my inmost calm."

Werner Mayer

TO SUFFER WOES WHICH HOPE

THINKS INFINITE;

TO FORGIVE WRONGS DARKER THAN

DEATH OR NIGHT; . . .

THIS, . . . IS TO BE

GOOD, GREAT AND JOYOUS,

BEAUTIFUL AND FREE;

THIS IS ALONE LIFE, JOY, EMPIRE

AND VICTORY.

Percy Bysshe Shelley

Happy Thirty-Fifth Anniversary

In February, Mary and Don had celebrated their thirty-fifth wedding anniversary. Then one afternoon a few weeks later, Don came home in the middle of the afternoon to announce that he wanted a divorce.

Mary's disbelief changed to anger and despair when she learned that for several months, Don had been dating one of his colleagues, a thirty-one-year-old accountant at the manufacturing company he now headed—the company Mary's father had built from the ground up. Wanting to keep the company in the family, Mary's father had turned the corporation over to Don a year before he retired.

Mary was filled with disbelief, anger, grief, and numbness. She was, however, fortunate enough to get an excellent divorce attorney and a superb counselor. Her minister was equally gifted in guiding her through grief and anger.

Despite this help, Mary had too much invested in their kids, their friends, the property they'd owned together, even the church she and Don had married in. Mary couldn't let go of linked, painful memories that only refueled her anger.

In April, when she was doing spring cleaning, she turned over the mattress and found Don's wedding band. "The creep," she thought. "He thought he could get rid of his guilt by hiding this!"

She hurled the ring across the room, and it landed on top of her dresser. Improbably, next to it lay her diamond engagement ring. She began to weep. But then she remembered some of the words from the Sunday scripture reading: "Forget the past. I have plans for you. To give you a future and a hope."

She decided that very moment to refashion the wedding band and her engagement ring into a cross to wear around her neck. Each time a negative memory threatened to plunge her into a vortex of anger and grief, she could touch it and repeat the words from scripture.

Mary took Don's wedding band and her diamond to the best jeweler she could find. He listened to her proposal and shook his head. "This ring's white gold."

"So what?"

"It's just that white gold is the hardest material to work with. It's just possible it won't melt down at all. And even if it does melt, it's too hard to form it just the way you want it."

"I'll take my chances," Mary said.

The next week the jeweler called Mary. "You won't believe this," he said. "I couldn't believe my eyes when it happened. I'm still sort of in shock."

Mary, thinking he was trying to tell her that the ring was really lost forever said, "Just tell me what happened."

"When I melted the white gold, it formed into a perfect cross!"

Mary wears her cross to this day. Now every time a disparaging thought comes into mind, she touches the cross and says, "Forget the past. I have plans for you. To give you a future and a hope."

TEACH US DELIGHT IN SIMPLE
  THINGS,
AND MIRTH THAT HAS NO BITTER
  SPRINGS;
FORGIVENESS FREE OF EVIL DONE,
AND LOVE TO ALL MEN 'NEATH THE
  SUN!

Rudyard Kipling

Priscilla J. Herbison received a Law Degree from the University of Minnesota and a Master's in Social Work from the University of Illinois. She currently serves as a professor at Saint Mary's University, where she is the program director of the Master's of Arts Human Development program.

In 1998, she received the George Christianson Award for Excellence in Education from Saint Mary's. The award, which honors outstanding leadership and integrity in higher education, has been given only five times in the University's history. Previous awards include an excellence in leadership award given by the Minnesota State University System and an excellence in teaching award from Saint Cloud State University in Minnesota.

Herbison lives in Minneapolis.